LOVE LIFE
AND
See Good Days

LOVE LIFE
AND
See Good Days

EMILY FREEMAN

DESERET
BOOK

Salt Lake City, Utah

For the fifty-three friends

who walked more than twenty-two miles.

That was a good day . . . one of my best days so far.

Photo credits: p. 10, Anan Kaewkhammul/Shutterstock; p. 11, Thinkstock; p. 26, Don Bayley/iStockphoto; p. 52, Kali Nine LLC/iStockphoto; p. 60, Gordon Dixon/ iStockphoto; p. 74, Silke Dietze/iStockphoto; p. 90, Jeffrey T. Kreulen/Shutterstock; p. 120, Hayley Alberts Photography. All other photos courtesy of the author.

Visit us at DeseretBook.com

Library of Congress Cataloging-in-Publication Data
Freeman, Emily, author.
    Love life, and see good days / Emily Freeman.
        pages cm
    Includes bibliographical references.
    Summary: Personal stories and scriptural insights offer suggestions for how to live a happier life.
    ISBN 978-1-60908-742-5 (hardbound : alk. paper)
    1. Happiness—Religious aspects—The Church of Jesus Christ of Latter-day Saints.
2. Christian life—Mormon authors. I. Title.
    BX8643.H35F74 2011
    248.4—dc23   2011022428

Printed in the United States of America
R. R. Donnelley, Crawfordsville, IN

10   9   8   7   6   5   4   3   2   1

CONTENTS

Introduction: Love Life, and See Good Days 1

Chapter 1: It's All in Your Perspective 9

Chapter 2: You Have Compassed This
Mountain Long Enough 27

Chapter 3: The Breaking of the Day
Has Found Me on My Knees. 37

Chapter 4: Live After the Manner of Happiness. . . 45

Chapter 5: I Knew . . . Yet I Would Not Know . . . 53

CONTENTS

Chapter 6: The Answer You Need 61

Chapter 7: My Heart Had Great Experience 75

Chapter 8: List What You Love 83

Chapter 9: Sowing in Tears—Reaping in Joy 91

Chapter 10: Specially This Day 101

Chapter 11: In Every Particular 111

Chapter 12: The Oil of Gladness 121

Conclusion: The Happy Book 129

Acknowledgments 135

Sources Cited 137

LOVE LIFE, AND
SEE GOOD DAYS

S everal years ago my husband, Greg, was called upon unexpectedly to travel to China. He would leave on December 26, and he wouldn't return home until the kids were back in school, which meant he would miss all of Christmas break. I was worried that the Christmas holiday would be ruined, so I decided to try to salvage it by taking my four kids up to Heber, a small town in the mountains of Utah, to stay in a cabin with some of my extended family. All of my kids had purchased season ski passes, so on our way to the cabin I stopped at Costco and bought some inexpensive passes for myself, thinking that if we went skiing every day, the time would pass more quickly.

1

That was a really good idea for the first two days, but by the end of the third day I could no longer walk. I don't ski that often, and I was using muscles I hadn't used for a very long time. When we returned home on that third day, I went right downstairs and put on my pajamas. Now, you need to know that my pajamas were cute! The pants were black flannel with red and cream stripes. I put on a red thermal shirt that matched, along with a cream-colored hoodie lined with fur.

After changing, I came upstairs to the kitchen to find that my mom had made white chicken chili for dinner. I love white chicken chili, but my kids don't. So I decided I would run down to the little market and buy chicken nuggets and French fries for them. That way everyone would be happy. My two sisters-in-law were sitting at the kitchen table, and I asked them, "Do you think it would be a big deal if I wore my pajamas to the grocery store?"

Their reply? "No, you will be there for five minutes; no one will even notice what you are wearing."

So I went to the store. As I drove into the parking lot, my cell phone started to ring. I answered as I walked into the store. Just inside the doors there was a Redbox machine, and I immediately noticed there was no one in line.

(As I am sure you are aware, that never happens.) I had three DVDs in my purse that needed to be returned, and I decided right then and there that this was my chance! I would return my DVDs while I finished talking on the phone.

I don't know if you know this, but the Redbox is the slowest machine ever invented. I stood there and patiently waited while each of the three DVDs was returned to its correct location in the box. By the time I was inserting the third DVD, a line had formed behind me. So, as I happened to be *first in line,* I decided to rent another movie for the night. To make things even better, the movie I wanted was right there on the first screen, so I selected it and waited for the movie to vend.

As I waited, a lady from the back of the line came up to me and asked, "Are you on the phone?" I looked at her and smiled and waved. *Of course* I was on my phone; she could see me talking into it. She continued, "Because you can't use this machine while you are talking on the phone." Now, in my defense, I thought she was telling me that you don't have to be a rocket scientist to use the Redbox machine, so I giggled and winked and waved again, and she got back in line.

My phone call ended just as my DVD came out of the slot. As I turned to leave, the woman from the back of the line returned and said, "You are rude! And you're *wearing your pajamas!*" I was mortified—and not quite sure what the correct response would be. I took my DVD and my cart and wandered into the grocery store, completely forgetting why I had come.

I walked aimlessly through the produce section, thinking to myself, *That lady is right, I should never have been talking on my cell phone while I was using the Redbox, I am rude.* By the time I got to the frozen food section I was saying to myself, *What were you thinking? You should never have come to the grocery store in your pajamas! How embarrassing!* By the time I got to the checkstand I was thinking, *If you would just act your age and hadn't gone skiing for three days in a row, you wouldn't have had to put on your pajamas at five o'clock in the afternoon.* By the time I got into the car I was thinking, *If you were a better mother you would have taught your kids to eat white chicken chili and then you wouldn't have had to come to the store for chicken nuggets and this would never have happened.* By the time I drove to the first stop sign I was in tears. Greg was in China and I had managed to ruin the entire Christmas holiday.

I walked into the house past my two sisters-in-law, who were still sitting at the kitchen table, and said, "The pajamas were a bad idea!" They watched me in silence as I opened the bags and started throwing frozen nuggets and fries onto two cookie sheets. Finally one of them asked what had happened. By the time I finished telling them, we were all hysterical with laughter. Through her laughter, one sister-in-law asked, "Why didn't you tell her, 'I *know* I am wearing my pajamas, I dressed myself'?" (Why is it you never think of the right thing to say in the moment?)

Isn't it amazing how one second we can be completely on top of the world, and all it takes is one person questioning our actions to make the whole world come crashing down around us? We begin to doubt ourselves. We become engulfed by discouragement. Sometimes these moments are funny, like when we wear our pajamas to the grocery store. But sometimes these moments are painful, like when we begin to doubt our abilities as a mother, a spouse, or a friend. We wonder if we can receive answers to prayer; we question our ability to understand the scriptures. All of a sudden it doesn't feel like a good day anymore. In those moments, it is hard to be happy.

How do we get through the times when it seems the

whole world is crashing down around us? How do we find the desire and outlook that will allow happiness to return? I love a scripture found in First Peter that says, "For he that will love life, and see good days . . . happy are ye" (1 Peter 3:10, 14). Peter's suggestion is simple but profound: love life, and see good days. I find it so interesting that the scripture does not tell us to love life and *have* good days. Sometimes I wish Peter had counseled us to have good days—I need more of those. Instead, the counsel is clear: *see* good days.

It is an interesting choice of words. We live in a society that is constantly reminding us to have a good day. We see that phrase written at the bottom of our restaurant receipts, hanging on the walls of our grocery stores, and even used as a salutation at the end of our e-mails. Interestingly, no one reminds us to *see* a good day.

I wonder how different our outlook on life would become if that became our motto. What if we trained ourselves to see good days?

I believe it is possible.

I believe it would be life changing.

I believe it would lead to more happiness.

But how is it done? I decided to turn to the scriptures

(my favorite place for advice) to try to find insight on how to see a good day. An amazing thing happened: I discovered that when you are trying to see good days, you are led to realize that the Lord filled the scriptures with happy verses. Lots of them. Within those verses I found twelve scriptures that have become simple suggestions to help me see good days. Each chapter of this book includes one of these scripture ideas. Perhaps they might become tools you can use in your own search to see a good day.

I don't know where you are in your life right now. Maybe the whole world has crashed down around you. On the other hand, maybe all of your ducks are sitting nicely in a row. (Mine aren't . . . you have to be able to *find* all your ducks before you can put them in a row.) No matter what your situation is, I hope these simple suggestions will lead you to discover some things in your life that you might not have recognized before. Happy things.

This is a handbook of happy thoughts.

Let them fill your heart and become a way of living so that you might love life and see good days.

Having eyes, see ye not?
How is it that ye do not understand?

MARK 8:18, 21

Chapter One

IT'S ALL IN YOUR PERSPECTIVE

The road to my children's school lies next to acres of farmland. One afternoon as I drove up that road, my eyes wandered across the fields approaching in front of my car. From my westward position it seemed the farmer had planted his crops quite randomly—green plants were sprouting up everywhere with absolutely no rhyme or reason. *What an awful mess,* I thought as my car approached the western border of the first field. Imagine my surprise once I got completely abreast of the field and looked out the passenger window to the right at perfectly lined rows running straight from north to south, with a carefully placed irrigation canal separating each row.

We passed by the first field, and as we approached the next one I turned to my daughter Megan and said, "Look up ahead at that field. What do you see?"

Her response was the same as mine, "A mess."

Once we were next to the field, I had her look again. "Now what do you see?"

A look of amazement crossed her face as she saw the crop growing in perfectly lined rows. "Mom, how did that happen?" she asked.

It is amazing what can happen if we simply change our point of view. Sometimes what once seemed a disastrous mess suddenly falls into place. Stepping back and looking

at things a different way allows us to realize that the situation is not as bad as it first appeared. In fact, sometimes it's good. Often all we need to do to see the good is simply redefine our perspective.

The scriptures teach, "He who hath faith to see shall see" (D&C 42:49). Learning to see good days might require a little faith and practice. Our outlook is often determined by our point of view.

I am convinced that all of us have moments when everything we perceive seems to be an awful mess. In these moments we must turn to the Lord. Focusing on Him will help us to receive a greater understanding of the situation.

He has counseled, "They seeing see not . . . but blessed are your eyes, for they see" (Matthew 13:13, 16).

In the eighth chapter of Mark we read of an experience when the disciples of Christ found themselves in need of a different perspective. On this particular day a great multitude had come to hear the Savior teach. The people had been with the Savior for three days, and they had not eaten during that time. The Savior was worried that if He sent them away fasting, they would faint before they could reach their homes.

It is clear that many of the people had traveled a long distance to hear the Lord speak. From the scriptures we learn that they were in the wilderness, far from a location where food might be purchased. Just as He had in a previous situation, Jesus asked the disciples how many loaves of bread they had. Then, in actions reminiscent of an earlier miracle, the Savior fed four thousand with seven loaves of bread and a few fishes.

I love the teaching moment that came after this miracle. Leaving a group of questioning Pharisees behind, Jesus entered a boat with the disciples to journey to the other side of the sea. Not long after they began their journey, the disciples realized they had forgotten to bring the bread that was remaining, and that within the ship there was only one loaf. As they discussed the situation, the Savior instructed them to "beware of the leaven of the Pharisees" (Mark 8:15). It was an interesting choice of words.

As is often the case, within one simple sentence the Lord had incorporated a complex lesson. This lesson is found in the word *leaven*. Leavening requires an agent, such as yeast. This leavening agent causes a reaction within the original dough, forming bubbles of gas, which lighten the finished product. When leaven is used, it causes the original dough to change—both in appearance and in flavor. Even just a small amount of leaven mixed into the dough will produce the desired effect throughout. The Savior was cautioning the disciples against the leaven of the Pharisees, who were filled with doubt, asking endless questions, seeking signs, tempting the Lord.

Not understanding, the disciples reasoned among themselves, and they finally decided the instruction from the Savior came because they had no bread. When Jesus heard this line of reasoning, He said, "Why reason ye, because ye have no bread? perceive ye not yet, neither understand? . . . Having eyes, *see ye not?*" (Mark 8:17, 18; emphasis added). Somehow the disciples had lost their focus. Forgetting the

Lord's ability to provide miracles within the ordinary, they were unable to see the good standing right in front of them and to understand its significance.

Trying to help them change their perspective, Jesus asked, "When I brake the five loaves among five thousand, how many baskets full of fragments took ye up? They say unto him, Twelve. And when the seven among four thousand, how many baskets full of fragments took ye up? And they said, Seven. And he said unto them, *How is it that ye do not understand?*" (Mark 8:19–21; emphasis added).

I can imagine His frustration. Just hours earlier, these men had witnessed a miracle. The Lord had taken seven loaves of bread and multiplied them to feed those who were wanting. It seemed His disciples were so focused on the problem of the one loaf of bread, they had completely forgotten that He with whom they traveled was capable of fulfilling their every need—if only they had faith. "We also too often misunderstand. . . . Seeing the scanty store in our basket, our little faith is busy with thoughts about . . . the one loaf which we have, forgetful that, where Christ is, faith may ever expect *all* that is needful" (Edersheim, *Life and Times of Jesus the Messiah,* 2:71; emphasis added).

In hard times, when things are not going as well as I

would hope, I try to focus again on the hand of the Lord in my life and to remember this cautionary phrase, "How is it that ye do not understand?" Maybe the only reason I don't understand is because I have forgotten to open my eyes to the miracles in the ordinary moments. I need to change my perspective from focusing on the one loaf to really seeing the Lord.

Sometimes this change of focus can be hard. It often requires help from the Lord. In my determination to acquire this gift, I have discovered three tools that have proven to be invaluable in changing my perspective. Hopefully these ideas will be as beneficial to you as they have been to me. Rather than just list the tools, I want to share them with you through life experiences. Perhaps, since each life experience contains a lesson within it, we could refer to them as life parables: The Parable of the Skunk, The Parable of the Porta-Potty, and the Parable of the Dandelions.

The Parable of the Skunk

One night, Greg was helping my brother-in-law paint his new home. I had spent the evening with my parents because I didn't want my youngest son, Josh, to breathe in the paint fumes. Josh was about eight months old at the time. He had been born with sleep apnea and now spent all of his sleeping hours hooked up to a special monitor that would alert us if he stopped breathing. Around ten o'clock that night, Greg called to say that they were finished painting. My dad offered to drive me to meet Greg over at the new house so we could all drive home together.

We pulled up and parked next to a large hedge across the street from the house. It was a beautiful summer evening, and although the sun had gone down, it was still very warm. I opened my door to get out and was immediately greeted by the thick, penetrating smell of a skunk. I hate skunks! I quickly checked around in the darkness to make sure the coast was clear and then opened the back door to start unloading Josh. Unplugging him from the monitor, I threw the diaper bag over one shoulder, lifted the breathing monitor strap over the other shoulder, and grabbed Josh's infant car seat to carry him from the car. I had just slammed the car door shut and walked around the back of the vehicle when I heard a noise. Immediately I knew what it was. "Dad," I whispered in pure panic, "the skunk is behind me!"

I was frozen in fear. I wasn't sure what the right thing to do might be. Were skunks like bees? If I stood still for long enough, would it leave me alone? My dad, on the other hand, bolted into action. With no concern for my welfare, he grabbed the car seat with Josh strapped in it and began running full speed down the center of the street. Now, I'm not stupid, and I wasn't going to face the skunk alone, so I took off running down the street behind him. As unbelievable as this might seem, I could hear the skunk running behind me in the darkness, chasing us down the street. I screamed after my dad, "It's following us! What should I do?" He just started running faster.

By now I was out of breath. I didn't know how much longer I could run with the heavy load I was carrying. As I approached the streetlight I decided to take a risk and turn around to see how close behind me the skunk was. Within the circle of light I immediately recognized the culprit. Instantly I fell to the ground, hysterical with laughter. My dad (who thought I had been skunked) stopped running and began to approach me slowly. "What is it?" he called out. "What's wrong?" I was laughing so hard it took me at least three minutes to answer.

The light had illuminated the whole situation. What I thought was a skunk was really the cord of Josh's monitor, which had been dragging five feet behind me since I had lifted it out of the car.

It is amazing what darkness can do. It has the unsettling effect of altering perception and creating a sense of unease. This unsettling effect happens to all of us at one time or another, and it is a reality that we need to acknowledge. Things seem to look more dire in the nighttime hours. We are all familiar with the admonition that it's always darkest just before the dawn.

Have you ever lain awake all night trying to solve a problem in your mind? Often these sleepless nights have led me to call on the Lord in prayer. When I can't sleep, I pray. Those dark, quiet hours allow uninterrupted time to counsel with the Lord. In Third Nephi we read, "Behold, I am . . . the light" (3 Nephi 15:9). In the darkest of hours, I have learned that the Savior really is a giver of light. When darkness surrounds us and seems to overtake us, we must do what Joseph Smith once did in a grove of trees—get down on our knees and pray.

Sometimes seeing a good day requires waiting for the sun to rise again. Often morning brings the peace and insight that elude us in the midnight hours. A key element for changing our point of view can be found in this beautiful scripture: "Weeping may endure for a night, but joy cometh in the morning" (Psalm 30:5).

Let the rising of the sun lift your spirit and enlighten your perspective. Spend the morning hours seeking some small portion of good amidst the darkness that surrounds you.

Maybe it's not the darkness of the night that is hindering your perception; maybe a sense of gloom is dimming your ability to see clearly. Try to shed some light on the situation. Turn to places and things that bring light. Morning hours, the scriptures, uplifting music, and time spent at the temple can help to illuminate your current circumstances.

The parable of the skunk teaches a simple but important lesson on perspective: If you can't see clearly now, wait for the light to come.

The Parable of the Porta-Potty

A good friend of mine went with her mother and sisters-in-law up to Midway, Utah, to shop at Swiss Days, an outdoor craft boutique. It was a girls' day out. After hours spent perusing items at the boutique, they decided it was time for a bathroom stop. They asked for directions to the restroom and eventually found themselves standing in front of a long row of Porta-Potties.

The women were not thrilled with this option, but since

there was no other alternative, they got in line. Once they were finished and had gathered back together, my friend's mother-in-law said, "That wasn't so bad. They have made these Porta-Potties so much nicer than they used to be. There is liquid sanitizer by the door, and it is so nice how they have that purse holder right next to the toilet seat."

All of the sisters looked at each other. None could remember seeing a purse holder in the stall. Then one sister burst out laughing and said, "Are you talking about the urinal?" A mass of hysteria ensued. Needless to say, the mother-in-law walked around for the rest of the day with a purse dripping with hand sanitizer.

I love this woman's point of view—where others saw a urinal, she saw a purse holder. It makes sense. Why include a urinal in a Porta-Potty? A purse holder would be so much more ingenious. She was doing her best to see something good in a situation that isn't normally pleasant.

But there is another important lesson we learn from this woman: She wasn't afraid to step back and laugh at her mistake.

This Porta-Potty example may seem trivial, but how many of us find ourselves in situations that we wouldn't consider pleasant? In those moments, hopefully we do our best to find the right perspective—to see the good. But every now and then our strokes of ingenuity don't turn out the way we had planned. Most likely, we won't be in a Porta-Potty when our moments of brilliance come, but we might find ourselves in a situation that we didn't choose to be in.

I think of a young mother trying to receive inspiration for one of her children because everything she's tried up to this point hasn't worked out the way she hoped; I think of a wife struggling to fit the pieces of her family's tight financial situation together; I think of a woman who hopes every day that she will be enough—in her job, in her calling, in her role at home—and perhaps even have some left over to fill her own bucket. And so we pray, and we try to see the inspiration, and we give our best to the situation.

Sometimes, even after our best effort, what once seemed like a good idea doesn't turn out the way we had hoped. All of us will experience discouragement, disappointment, and even failure. In order to change our perspective, we have to rise above the problems and learn from the mistakes. Things aren't always going to go the way we plan or think they should. It's okay to step back, reanalyze the situation, and maybe even laugh.

There have been so many situations in my life in which

I could have chosen to cry hard or to laugh hard—and sometimes I have found myself doing both at the same time. I have said more than once, "In a couple of days I will be able to look back at this awful experience and laugh . . . if I can just get through it now." Laughter is healing. It doesn't mean that what you are going through isn't serious or real—it just makes some of those painful moments a little easier to bear. Having a perspective that allows us to laugh and make the best of whatever situation we are in is often a key to seeing good days.

The Parable of the Dandelions

One weekend my girls and I took a drive together. We passed through acres and acres of farmland. My eyes were drawn to the overwhelming number of dandelions that had taken over the fields. The green landscape was dotted with a mixture of bright yellow flowers and white, fluffy balls of seeds.

We had spent weeks trying to kill the dandelions in our own yard, and I thought about what a job that farmer would have trying to clear those weeds from his landscape.

My daughters saw something different: acres and acres of dandelion fluff just waiting to be blown from the stem.

A thousand weeds or a thousand wishes.

It's all in your perspective.

My girls were able to discern something good in an object most of us view as an irritant or a bother. The lesson in this parable is so clearly defined: Our eyes see what we want them to see.

This lesson becomes so much more profound when applied to real-life situations. Think of your relationships with members of your family; consider your outlook on your current life situation; reflect on the private conversations you have with yourself about who you are and who you are becoming. What is it that you focus on? What do you see?

If our focus is to see good even when that good part might be hard to uncover—if that is the principle that motivates our vision—it can completely change our view. One key to seeing good days is to learn how to discern the good in every situation we find ourselves in.

Life has taught me that this kind of discernment is a gift. Some of us are born with this ability; others might have to pray and work diligently to receive it. Elder Stephen L Richards said, "This gift, when highly developed arises largely out of an acute sensitivity to impressions—spiritual impressions, if you will—to read under the surface . . . to find the good that may be concealed. The highest type of discernment is that which perceives in others and uncovers for them their better natures, the good inherent within them" (in Conference Report, April 1950, 162). Let what you see be governed by a desire to uncover something better, to recognize the concealed good that is inherent within.

To see a good day, change your perspective. Look at things in a different light. Laugh. Uncover the good that may be concealed. Let your perspective allow you to focus on the Lord. Through Him, understanding will come.

To see a good day . . . change your perspective.

Ye have compassed this
mountain long enough.
The Lord thy God hath been with thee.
Now rise up, said I, and get you over.
Rise ye up, take your journey.

DEUTERONOMY 2:3, 7, 13, 24

Chapter Two

YOU HAVE COMPASSED
THIS MOUNTAIN
LONG ENOUGH

Right off the bat we should address an important fact—some days are bad. And sometimes those bad days last for weeks and even months at a time. Bad days are real. You can't pretend they aren't happening. You can't pretend your heart isn't heavy. You can't pretend that you are capable of doing anything more on those days than just surviving. I know about those days.

I will never forget the advice a friend gave me during a really trying time in my life. I was having trouble processing my emotions, keeping track of the tiny details—it seemed that even the daily tasks I had always been able to stay on top of had become too much. My friend told me

I needed to set everything aside for a while and focus on what was essential. Then he asked me, "What is the most essential thing you have to do to get through the next few days?"

Immediately my mind focused on all of the aspects of my life that were slipping through the cracks while I tried desperately to hold myself together. He must have been able to see my mind trying to catch the fragments of the sky that were falling down around me because before I could answer, he prompted, "There's only one essential. Breathe. That is the most essential thing you have to do to get through the next few days. Just breathe."

He was right. Breathing was essential.

I knew how to breathe.

I could do that.

I love a story that was shared in general conference several years ago about a man named Henry Clegg Jr. Henry joined the Church in Preston, England, and then decided to immigrate to Utah. His wife, Hannah, and their two young boys came with him. Unfortunately, Henry's parents were too feeble to make the journey, and so he said goodbye to them in England, knowing he would never see them again.

Crossing the plains was a difficult journey. Hannah became sick with cholera and died. She was laid to rest beside the trail in an unmarked grave. What an awful morning that must have been, as Henry continued the journey westward knowing he was leaving his wife behind. At six o'clock that same evening, Henry's youngest son died. Henry's account describes how he went back to the grave of his wife, carefully unburied her, placed their son into her arms, and reburied them together. Then he returned to the journey, walking five miles to join the wagon train. Henry was also at death's door, suffering from cholera, with over a thousand miles left to walk. But still he continued on.

I find it heartbreaking that Henry stopped writing in his journal for several weeks after losing his dear wife and tiny son. I imagine his emotions and his illness exhausted his reserves. Perhaps he too understood the principle of focusing on the bare essentials. The first two words Henry used when he finally started writing in his journal again were, "Still moving" (see Gayle M. Clegg, "The Finished Story," 14).

Not leaping, showered in joy, or overwhelmed with celebration. Just breathing. Still moving.

Have you ever had one of those moments? A moment

when all of your energy was focused on simply surviving? In those deeply personal moments, it seems our spirits instinctively draw closer to the Savior. Often leaning on Him is the only way to get through the trial that seems to overwhelm us. His grace is an enabling power. He offers a divine means of help. Through Him we receive strength and assistance that we wouldn't be able to maintain if left only to our own means (see LDS Bible Dictionary, s.v. "grace").

During one of the hardest times of my life, I stumbled upon a scripture that I clung to for many months. It said, "As yet I am as strong . . . now therefore give me this mountain . . . the Lord will be with me" (Joshua 14:11, 12). I love the message of this scripture. I am not afraid of the mountain ahead, as long as I know the Lord will be with me.

Each of us will experience mountain moments in our lives. These are not small, inconsequential obstacles, particularly if we are the ones who are trying to conquer the summit. Oftentimes in these situations others watch us from a distance and seem to have a hard time visualizing the mountain we are individually trying to climb.

You have probably heard the familiar adage "You are

making a mountain out of a molehill." But what happens if the mountain really is a mountain? What do we do then?

Many years ago, Moses was trying to lead the people of Israel to the promised land. They took their journey into the wilderness by way of the Red Sea and compassed Mount Seir for many days. Finally the Lord spoke to Moses and said, "Ye have compassed this mountain long enough: turn you northward" (Deuteronomy 2:3).

I am intrigued by this thought.

In my mind I can hear the Lord saying, "You have journeyed through this place long enough. It is time to walk away from it. Leave it behind now. Let it go."

Life is full of mountain moments. Within those moments we will pray for direction, seek for understanding, and long for the promised end. Our mountain moments may cause reason for mourning; we may plead with the Lord to give us strength. Sometimes those moments seem to last forever. The Lord allows time for mourning, for growing, for stretching, for gaining strength. But there will come a day, in the midst of these experiences, when we will hear the quiet whisper from the Lord, "Ye have compassed this mountain long enough."

The Lord told Moses that the walking away wouldn't

necessarily be easy. In fact, others would lie in the path. His counsel was clear: "Meddle not with them" (Deuteronomy 2:5). It seems that the Lord is teaching an important principle here. Sometimes we have to let go of what is holding us back in order to reach the promised end. When the Spirit prompts us to move on, we must somehow move past the painful things that seem to overwhelm and constrain us. This requires allowing the healing to come. Sometimes this requires forgiveness. At other times we might lean heavily on repentance. Always we must find courage.

There is another important lesson we learn from this chapter. Throughout this mountain moment, the people of Israel had not traveled alone. Moses told them, "For the Lord thy God . . . knoweth thy walking through this great wilderness: these forty years the Lord thy God hath been with thee; thou hast lacked nothing" (Deuteronomy 2:7).

Think about the mountain moments you have journeyed through, the great wilderness places of your life. Comfort fills my heart when I realize the Lord *knows* about the mountain, and He *knows* the walking through the wilderness. He knows. And not only does He see us walking through, He is there with us.

Looking back at the mountain and wilderness moments of my life with a perspective focused on Him, I realize a powerful truth: As empty and heavy as my heart was, I lacked nothing. The Lord filled the empty places and lifted my heavy heart.

Often these mountain moments and wilderness places provide some of life's greatest miracles. Within the journey we are able to witness moments with the Lord, if our eyes are only open to see.

The chapter of scripture ends with two important messages strung in the midst: "Now rise up, said I, and get you over," and "Rise ye up, take your journey" (Deuteronomy 2:13, 24). Perhaps the only way we can move through the hardest days and on to the promised end is to follow this counsel and rise above them. Most often we will not have the power to do this on our own. The Lord knows how to lift. He has the capacity to strengthen us until we can move forward again on our own.

We won't always *have* good days. But even in the midst of life's most overwhelming challenges, we can *see* good days by just breathing, still moving, rising above, and recognizing that the Lord will not leave us to journey alone. The Lord *is* completely aware of our journey through every great wilderness. He will guide us beyond the mountain moments. Even on our very worst days—especially on those days—He is with us. He will make sure that we lack nothing.

He will help us to see a good day.

To see a good day . . . rise above and continue your journey, knowing the Lord is with you.

The stone which the builders refused is
become the head stone of the corner.
This is the Lord's doing; it is
marvellous in our eyes.
This is the day which the Lord hath made;
we will rejoice and be glad in it.

PSALM 118:22–24

Chapter Three

THE BREAKING OF
THE DAY HAS FOUND
ME ON MY KNEES

On a rocky shoreline that separates the land from the sea, there is a man who balances stones. It is painstaking work and often tedious. Hours of effort are required to complete the task. I watched him one day, intrigued by his patience, in awe of his ability to align the rocks in such a way that each rock not only balanced on the one below but could also support the weight of the one above.

His hands were steady, carefully placing the rock just so and then attempting to let go. If the rock would not balance, he would move it in tiny increments, almost so small that you couldn't even notice the adjustment. Then he would try to remove his hands again. The seconds dragged into minutes, and honestly I am not sure how long I sat there, transfixed by his endeavor, my eyes drawn to his hands and the possibility that lay at his fingertips.

Finally it was done. Stone upon stone stood precariously, some piled up to eight stones high—each stack reaching upward to the sky. When he had finished, the stone balancer removed his hands and stepped away to view the masterpiece. The watchers clapped in their delight as the balancer stood back—content.

As I watched, I wondered to myself how that man had obtained that talent. Had he come across that rocky beach and recognized immediately the opportunity that lay within? How did he know which rocks to use? What was it that allowed him to see a masterpiece of balance where others just saw a bed of rocks? This man had turned an area of the world that most people passed by without a second glance into an exhibit where people stopped to photograph his work. He saw the good.

What if we approached each day with the eyes of the stone balancer? Then, instead of seeing just *another* day, we might see a day that holds great possibilities for good within it.

In order to do this, we will have to learn from the stone balancer's techniques. First, because there will be many stones to choose from, we must identify the ones we want to use. Some of these stones might include responsibilities like work or family care. The use of those stones is mandatory. Other stones are optional; we get to choose these ourselves. They might include service, quiet time, or exercise. Amidst these stones of choice, perhaps we might choose to add scripture study, heartfelt prayer, and meditation.

The second thing the stone balancer does is to start building with the stones he has chosen, one stone upon the other. Sometimes a stone doesn't fit—no matter how hard he tries, the balance can't be achieved. At such a time he has to set that stone aside and choose another. The same is true in our lives. Some activities won't fit right into the balance of our day. It might not necessarily be because we have chosen the wrong activity, but maybe we are putting too much time there, or possibly not enough. It's okay to set the stone aside for a bit and study why it doesn't seem to be working. With enough patience and adjustment, the answer will come.

The last thing the stone balancer does is to step back and view his masterpiece—to look over what he has accomplished. It is practice and understanding that allows him to create each masterpiece. At the end of each day, we too can look back to see what we have accomplished. But how do we obtain the practice and understanding that will allow us to become masters at balancing?

Think of the day you had yesterday. How much time did you spend nurturing? How about pondering the scriptures? Were you able to spend time in prayer? Did you exercise? Did you have an uplifting conversation with a friend? What other stones did you gather and stack carefully into your pile? Looking back at the whole of the day, do you ever find yourself wondering when it is "weighed in the balances" if it is "found wanting" (Daniel 5:27)? What can we do so that our days are not found wanting?

Perhaps we might begin each day as President Spencer W. Kimball suggested: "The breaking of the day has found me on my knees" ("Breaking of the Day," 52). Perhaps we could pray for guidance as we struggle to balance our roles as caretakers, nurturers, or providers. Ours might be a prayer for strength as we consider the burdens that will be balanced within our carefully constructed pile. Perhaps we might pray for an increase in charity, or for opportunities to act as instruments in the Lord's hands.

The Lord will open our eyes to recognize the good that lies within the day ahead of us if we just take the time to ask.

Always, within each day we must turn to the scriptures. The stories contained therein hold keys to discovering balance. If we search the scriptures for ideas to create balance in our lives, we will find answers to our prayers.

Sometimes when I am overwhelmed with my responsibilities and the tasks on my to-do list seem destined to remain forever unaccomplished, I try to remember a scripture in the book of Isaiah. Speaking of the Savior, it asks, "Who hath measured the waters in the hollow of his hand, and meted out heaven with the span, and comprehended the dust of the earth in a measure, and weighed the mountains in scales, and the hills in a balance? Who hath directed the Spirit of the Lord?" (Isaiah 40:12–13).

I love to picture the Savior with the water of the earth cupped in one hand while the other hand spans the expanse of heaven. He knows instantly how to measure out the dust and to balance the mountains and hills. If the Savior can handle all of that, I know that He can help me balance the details of my life. If I turn to Him for help, the Spirit will direct me, and through Him answers will come.

Balance will become easier to achieve as we approach

the day with prayer as our foundation and with scripture study placed carefully above it. If we start there, we will not be working alone. The Lord will be our partner. He will help us to choose the best stones; He will steady our hands; He will guide our progress.

A scripture in Psalms reads, "The stone which the builders refused is become the head stone of the corner. This is the Lord's doing; it is marvellous in our eyes. This is the day which the Lord hath made; we will rejoice and be glad in it" (Psalm 118:22–24). The footnotes help us to understand that the stone the builders refused became the cornerstone, representative of Jesus Christ, "himself being the chief corner stone" (Ephesians 2:20). Above all else, He is the most important stone in our day. Although others may reject Him, our choosing to include Him in the balance of our day will make a noticeable difference. Through Him we will be led to see that this day "is the day which the Lord hath made;" and "we will rejoice and be glad in it" (Psalm 118:24).

Then, after the sun has set, as the stars sparkle along the horizon and fill the night sky, perhaps we will find ourselves in the same place we were when the dawn broke—on our knees. In this moment of prayer, which becomes the culmination of our day, we might find ourselves offering a devotion of gratitude for the balance that has begun to fill our life.

Within each day there are great possibilities that lie at our fingertips. If we turn each day over to the Lord and balance our efforts on a foundation of prayer and scripture study, something miraculous will begin to happen. At the end of the day we will be able to look back at what we have accomplished and see a small masterpiece. Within that moment there will be gladness and rejoicing as we see the good within. We might even clap in our delight as we look back—content.

To see a good day . . . make prayer and scripture study the foundation.

We lived after the manner of happiness.

2 NEPHI 5:27

Chapter Four

LIVE AFTER THE
MANNER OF HAPPINESS

I have a four-by-six-inch photograph hanging on the
blackboard in my kitchen as a constant reminder. It
is a photo of my dear friend Verda, who had just returned
from a five-mile snowmobile trip when the picture was
snapped. Verda is sitting on the back of the snowmobile in
her blue parka and grey leggings, an orange scarf pulled up
carefully around her face. She is completely dusted in fine,
white powder from head to toe.

You are probably wondering why I keep this particular
photo as a reminder, and what it could possibly be a reminder of. Perhaps you would be intrigued to know that
my friend Verda is ninety-nine years old. Really. She is.

And she recently took a five-mile snowmobiling trip and got completely dusted in snow.

This photo reminds me to live. Every second. To enjoy every moment. To be spontaneous. To make memories.

We live in a generation of life quotes. We are surrounded by clever snippets meant to motivate us. Some of my favorites include quotes that encourage us to make the most of our lives: "Live out loud." "Live what you love." "Live your best life." The Book of Mormon contains a one-liner that would fit in perfectly here: Live "after the manner of happiness" (2 Nephi 5:27).

My friend Verda knows how to do this. I love her optimism and her zeal for life. Her journey has not been an easy one, but she chooses happiness. Her attitude is contagious. She is someone people love to be around. Speaking of the women who would live in the latter days, President Spencer W. Kimball said that the women of the Church would be seen as "distinct and different—in happy ways" ("Role of Righteous Women," 104). Verda is one of those women—she is distinct and different in happy ways. She lives after the manner of happiness.

President Thomas S. Monson once shared the story of a woman named Borghild Dahl. "She was born in

Minnesota in 1890 of Norwegian parents and from her early years suffered severely impaired vision. She had a tremendous desire to participate in everyday life despite her handicap and, through sheer determination, succeeded in nearly everything she undertook. Against the advice of educators, who felt her handicap was too great, she attended college, receiving her bachelor of arts degree from the University of Minnesota. She later studied at Columbia University and the University of Oslo. She eventually became the principal of eight schools in western Minnesota and North Dakota.

"She wrote the following in one of the 17 books she authored: 'I had only one eye, and it was so covered with dense scars that I had to do all my seeing through one small opening in the left of the eye. I could see a book only by holding it up close to my face and by straining my one eye as hard as I could to the left.'

"Miraculously, in 1943—when she was over 50 years old—a revolutionary procedure was developed which finally restored to her much of the sight she had been without for so long. A new and exciting world opened up before her. She took great pleasure in the small things most of us take for granted, such as watching a bird in flight, noticing the light reflected in the bubbles of her dishwater, or observing the phases of the moon each night. She closed one of her books with these words: 'Dear . . . Father in heaven, I thank Thee. I thank Thee.'

"Borghild Dahl, both before and after her sight was restored, was filled with gratitude for her blessings. In 1982, two years before she died, at the age of 92 her last book was published. Its title: *Happy All My Life*" ("Finding Joy in the Journey," 87).

These two remarkable women took what life brought them and decided to choose happiness. Perhaps we could learn from their example and add some of these phrases to our list of motivational snippets: *Live after the manner of happiness; be distinct and different in happy ways; choose happiness; happy all my life.*

The Book of Mormon references three different societies whose inhabitants lived after the manner of happiness. If you read through the chapters describing their lifestyle, it becomes quickly apparent that each of these societies had three things in common: they knew how to work, they lived without contention, and they kept the commandments in all things. It is a simple formula for happiness.

I love how each society is described. In the beginning

of the Book of Mormon, after Nephi and his people left Laman and Lemuel and fled into the wilderness, Nephi described their day-to-day conditions and said, "And it came to pass that we lived after the manner of happiness" (2 Nephi 5:27).

Later, in the book of Alma, we read of Captain Moroni. His people were described as "those who were faithful in keeping the commandments of the Lord." Because of their faithfulness they were "delivered at all times," and Mormon writes, "Behold there never was a happier time among the people of Nephi . . . than in the days of Moroni, yea, even at this time" (Alma 50:22, 23). Even in a time of war, the people had learned a formula for happiness.

Last we read in Fourth Nephi of the people who lived in a time without envy, strife, tumult, lying, or murder. The scriptures state, "And surely there could not be a happier people among all the people who had been created by the hand of God. . . . And how blessed were they! For the Lord did bless them in all their doings" (4 Nephi 1:16, 18).

Much can be learned from a study of these three chapters. The strategies for happiness found in them are applicable to each of us. By learning from these Book of Mormon examples, perhaps we too can be blessed in all our doings, be delivered at all times, and live after the manner of happiness.

Recently I went to visit Verda. We sat on her family-room couch and talked. As I prepared to leave, she told me, "Life is wonderful. The world is beautiful. Enjoy the journey." I left her home smiling. My spirit had been lifted. My association with Verda has blessed me to see good days. One of the greatest pieces of wisdom I know about seeing good days is something I learned from her example and can be summed up in two words—*live happy.*

To see a good day . . .
live happy.

I said I never had known much of these things; but behold, I mistake, for I have seen much of his mysteries and his marvelous power. . . . I knew . . . yet I would not know.

ALMA 10:5–6

Chapter Five

I KNEW . . . YET I WOULD NOT KNOW

O ne of my favorite summertime activities is to watch a parade. I love a good parade from start to fin-ish—the sirens; the standing up as the flag passes by; the princesses; the floats; the candy. I am particularly happy if I am sitting under the shade of a huge maple tree during those experiences. Parades are one of my favorite parts of summer.

Many years ago Brad Wilcox told the story of a small boy who went to watch a parade with his father. They had planned for the big day weeks in advance, and when the an-ticipated occasion arrived they pushed through the crowd, trying to get as close as they could to the front, and then prepared to watch the parade. The sirens came, signaling the beginning of what the father hoped would be a wonderful hour spent with his son, but soon his enthusiasm was crushed. His small son began to cry. The dad told him, "Be happy. This is the parade. We've been looking forward to this for weeks. Try to enjoy it." But the son continued to sob.

Finally the father bent down to speak to his small child and discovered an important reality. The child could not see the parade. Directly in his line of vision were the legs and chairs and bodies of the people sitting in the rows in front of them. He could hear that the parade had started, but he was totally missing the event because he could not see it. The father lifted the boy up onto his shoulders where his view would not be obstructed, and then together they enjoyed the parade.

In our attempt to see good days, our focus becomes essential. If that focus becomes impeded, if we let other things get in the way, it is hard to recognize the good that is happening all around us. Sometimes it requires heaven's help to lift us high enough to look past the distractions and see the good again.

I love to read the story of Amulek, a man of no small reputation, with many kindreds and friends, and much money (see Alma 10:4). Amulek was obviously a man who was very blessed, and yet he tells us, "Nevertheless, *after all this,* I never have known much of the ways of the Lord, and his . . . marvelous power. I said I never had known much of these things; but behold, *I mistake,* for I *have* seen much of his . . . marvelous power. . . . Nevertheless, I did harden my heart . . . ; therefore *I knew* concerning these things, *yet I would not know*" (Alma 10:5–6; emphasis added).

Even though he was surrounded by blessings, Amulek did not open his eyes to see the good things. It wasn't until the Lord opened his eyes that Amulek recognized blessings unmeasured and said, "He hath blessed mine house, he hath blessed me, and my women, and my children, and my father and my kinsfolk; yea, even all my kindred hath he blessed, and the blessing of the Lord hath rested upon us" (Alma 10:11).

I sometimes wonder if we fall into the trap of Amulek. Do we get so caught up in the day-to-day happenings of life that we forget to see God in the details? Maybe if we could just stop for a little while and remove the distractions, we would begin to discover miracles in the ordinary moments of our lives.

Many years ago I read a poem with a poignant message. The image of this message has never left my thoughts, and I often find myself reflecting on it as I try to remember to focus on the wonders of God around me.

> *The boy whispered,*
> *"God, speak to me."*
> *And a bird sang.*
> *The boy yelled,*
> *"God, I can't hear you."*
> *And thunder roared.*
> *Still, the boy did not hear.*
> *So, the boy said,*
> *"God, let me see you."*
> *And a star shone.*
> *But the boy did not see.*
> *He cried out,*
> *"God, perform a miracle."*
> *And a child was born.*
> *But the boy did not know.*
> *The boy became angry and screamed,*
> *"God, let me know you are near!"*
> *God bent down and touched the boy's shoulder,*
> *And the boy brushed the butterfly from his shoulder*
> *And walked away*
> *Unknowingly.*
>
> *Author Unknown*

This poem is inspiring to me. Every time I hear it, I want more than ever to change my focus so that I can see the good that a loving Heavenly Father is sending me. But I have come to realize that sometimes finding this focus can be hard.

The first decade of married life was really difficult for my husband and me. Things kept going wrong. Just when it seemed one thing was resolved, something new and foreboding was waiting around the corner. Together Greg and I learned the meaning of terms like *cancer, diabetes,* and *CPR.* Our experience expanded to include severe migraines and depression. Hospitals became like a vacation home for us— it seemed that we were scheduling a trip there at least once every six months. Our life lessons included realizing that you don't always get what you hope for, and sometimes you have to set aside your dreams knowing you won't come back to pick them up later. I can remember turning to Greg after one particularly hard day and saying, "My life was really great until I met you; after that, everything seemed to go downhill." We laughed and laughed. That was the state of our life.

It got to the point where I found myself constantly wondering what could possibly happen next. I didn't look forward to the future with anticipation; instead I looked ahead with a constant sense of foreboding. Then one day I realized I wasn't happy anymore. I wasn't the cheerful person I had always been. I had forgotten what it felt like to feel joy. I had lost focus.

I knew I had to do something to pull myself out of the pit I had gotten into. Part of the solution included prayers in the late hours of the night, where I learned I could receive strength beyond my own to help me carry the burdens that were mine. But I also needed a daytime solution. One evening at a small craft boutique I found the answer—a blessing jar.

I brought the small green jar home and placed it in the middle of the kitchen table, where I would see it every single day. The word *blessings* written across the front of the jar became a constant reminder that I needed to change my focus. I opened my eyes to see the hand of the Lord in my life, to see Him in the details, and then I wrote down those moments on tiny pieces of paper and placed them in the jar. It's amazing what happens when you do that. I found blessings everywhere: in a phone call from a friend, a favorite song on the radio, and within my daily scripture study. Looking back, I realize the Lord was sending blessings all along; I just couldn't see them. I knew, yet I would not know. I had walked away unknowingly.

The blessings were in the details.

They had been there all along.

Many decorations have come and gone from our home in the two decades that we have been married. One still holds a prominent place of honor. It is the blessing jar. I find myself turning to it on a regular basis when I need to find focus again.

Perhaps you would like to create your own blessing jar. Find a prominent place for the jar somewhere in your home. Let the jar become a constant reminder of your desire to remember that God is in the details.

Learning to recognize the blessings of the Lord in the details of our lives can help us to see good days.

***

To see a good day . . . look for God within the details.

But prayer was made without ceasing. . . .
The Lord hath sent his angel,
And hath delivered me.

ACTS 12:5, 11

Chapter Six

THE ANSWER
YOU NEED

I t wasn't the answer I had expected, nor was it the answer I wanted to hear.

It was the day before we were leaving for our ward girls camp. The weather forecast for the upcoming week was awful—rain, rain, and then, as if that weren't enough, more rain. We gathered as a group of leaders to discuss the last-minute details and to pray for the obvious solution—sunshine. As we prepared to leave the church building, I unexpectedly ran into one of our stake Young Women leaders in the foyer. "Are you ready for tomorrow?" she asked.

"As ready as we can be," I replied, "but we could use your prayers for good weather."

Her answer left me speechless: "I will pray for the weather you need."

What was that all about? I didn't want the weather we *needed*, I wanted sunshine. The camp we had signed up for offered canoeing, horseback riding, archery, basketball, and swimming. In case it isn't readily apparent, those are all outdoor activities. Besides, we were sleeping in tents . . . need I say more?

And so the adventure began. We left the valley just as the sun began to rise over the mountains, and we traveled an hour to our destination, driving the last twelve miles over a bumpy dirt road. Just as we pulled into the ranch, the rain began to fall. The Scout trailer, with all of our belongings and tents, was due to arrive two hours later. We went to lunch and then to the lake. By the time two hours had passed, we were dripping wet. Many other groups had arrived at the camp, bringing with them some bad news: the twelve-mile dirt road was barely passable because of the rain, and some of the cars had almost slid into the lake in their attempt to reach the ranch. So another leader and I set off in a four-wheel-drive truck to rescue Sister Remington and the Scout trailer—prized possession of the Lehi Thirty-Third Ward.

Our truck barely made it down the steep hill leading

out of the ranch. The wheels were twelve inches deep in sticky mud, and we found ourselves fishtailing across the washed-out road, over the skinny, sloping bridge, and around the lake, where two men from the ranch advised us that with road conditions like this, Sister Remington and the trailer probably weren't going to make it to girls camp. That was going to present a problem. The only supplies we currently had with us were the clothes on our backs. Thankfully, just five minutes later, we looked up to see Sister Remington rounding the bend in the truck, slowly crawling along the slippery road.

Getting the trailer where it needed to be would mean traveling over the perilous one-lane bridge, along the washed-out road—which was now lying under six inches of water—and up a steep incline that led to the ranch. As if that weren't enough, there was another problem: so many cars had gotten stuck traveling up the steep hill into the ranch that an extremely deep rut had formed on the right side, which happened to be the safest side of the road. This meant we would have to drive the car and trailer as far to the left as we could, avoiding the rut, hugging the edge of the slender road that dropped off in a steep incline ending at the lake. Honestly, I was 30 percent worried for our safety and 70 percent worried that my legacy would be to be known as the camp director who let the Scout trailer, prized possession of the Lehi Thirty-Third Ward, roll down the mountain and fall into the bottom of the lake.

We counseled together for a half an hour with the men from the ranch about what we should do and finally decided to go for it. All of our tents, food, and clothing were nestled safe and dry within that trailer. Without the trailer we would not have enough dry storage for our food and equipment. Even if we carried the tents up the hill on foot, there just would not be enough tent space for everything else. Sister Remington, Sister Bennett, and I started to pray while the director of the camp gathered all the men and teenage boys who ran the camp to line both sides of the road. Some would try to steer us away from the rut, and some were there to guide us as far to the left as possible without sending us rolling down the mountain.

I decided to ride with Sister Remington as moral support. We had made it a little more than halfway up the incline, pedal to the floor, the truck giving everything it had, when Sister Remington whispered, "The trailer is pulling us down the side of the mountain." I looked down the incline to the lake and then looked up to see those men and teenage boys, spaced about ten feet apart, lining each side of the slippery road, literally cheering us on—fists in the air, hope on their faces. And somehow it was enough. The truck pulled the trailer around the rut and up into the horse pasture where we would stay.

We set up the tents in the rain. We roasted marshmallows during a small break in the rain. And we went to bed with the sound of rain falling on the tents. We prayed for sunshine with every prayer, but nonetheless, it rained the whole time. All three days. Couldn't go in the lake for fear of lightning. Tried archery, but the arrows were too slippery. Tried horseback riding, too. I wonder if you know that when a trail is really wet and slippery, a horse will sit down on its hind legs and slide down the mountain in a sitting position, even with a rider on its back. We decided that probably was not safe. So we spent the entire camp in a plywood gazebo, and, through inspiration and prayer, we improvised.

Within those walls we spoke of the Young Women Values. We researched women in the scriptures who lived those values. We each tried to determine which value was most like us and wrote it down so that we would remember it. Then we tried to think of two words that would allow us to better live that value. We had amazing experiences we hadn't planned on, all within the walls of a partially constructed gazebo.

Did I mention it rained at girls camp?

By Wednesday afternoon the Duchesne Sheriff's Department had closed the dirt road on both sides of the camp, pronouncing the driving conditions too dangerous—a propane tanker had slid off the road. On Thursday morning the road had still not been opened, and I started to panic that we might have to stay at girls camp forever. I love girls camp, but not for the whole summer.

After counseling together with the other leaders, Sister Bennett and I went to the truck to call my husband, Greg, on her satellite phone. I begin the conversation by saying, "Greg, we are in trouble . . ." I didn't get one more word of explanation out before he said, "The priesthood is already on the way; they left at seven o'clock this morning." Immediately I felt relief wash over me. A rescue had been planned. I knew the priesthood brothers would know how to save us from our predicament. We packed up our entire camp and then we patiently waited.

Within two hours the men were there, and an hour after that we were on our way down the mountain, minus the camp trailer. (Don't worry, Scout lovers; we retrieved it three weeks later, *after* it finally stopped raining.)

After it was all over, I spent some time considering our experience. At first glance, it seemed like everything was a failure. We spent more time in the gazebo than we did on the canoes, the horses, or the basketball court. We made s'mores (my favorite part of girls camp) on only one of the three evenings, during a thirty-minute break in the clouds. We didn't have any exciting outdoor camping pictures; every backdrop was the cement floor and plywood walls of the gazebo. I wondered why our prayers had not been answered.

But interestingly, as we left for home, and throughout the next week, I kept hearing the Young Women say, "This was the best girls camp ever." As I listened to their testimonies, I was intrigued by what they had learned from the experience. They spoke of how prayers for safety had been answered. They testified of the strength of the priesthood and talked about how grateful they were for the men in our ward who honored that responsibility. They shared gratitude for what they had learned about the values that they hadn't known before.

Suddenly it became extremely clear to me that the prayer offered by a stake Young Women leader before the week had even begun had indeed been answered: We *had* been given the weather we needed. It had allowed for an experience that increased testimonies, and no amount of sunshine or fun could compare with that.

Looking back, I realized that we had prayed desperately with every prayer that the girls would have a great experience and that we would have the weather that would make it possible. And all along, the Lord was in the process of answering our prayer—we just hadn't realized it. When I recognized that the Lord had sent the answer we *needed,* I was finally able to see the good.

In Acts, chapter twelve, we learn an interesting lesson on prayer. The chapter begins with the news that King Herod had killed James, the brother of John, with a sword. Because the killing of James pleased the Jews so greatly, Herod took Peter into custody also. It was his intention to bring Peter before the people just after Easter. We read, "Peter therefore was kept in prison: but prayer was made *without ceasing* of the church unto God for him" (Acts 12:5; emphasis added).

The night before Peter was to be brought forth before the people, something remarkable happened. Peter was in prison. There were four quaternions of soldiers to guard him. He slept between two soldiers, bound with two chains, with more men guarding the door outside. Meanwhile, many of the Saints had gathered together at the house of Mary to pray.

That night, an angel of the Lord came to Peter in prison, "and he smote Peter on the side, and raised him up, saying, Arise up quickly. And his chains fell off from his hands" (Acts 12:7). The angel told Peter to get dressed and follow him out of the prison.

It all happened so quickly that Peter thought it was a dream. The scriptures tell us that when Peter "was come to himself, he said, Now I know of a surety, that the Lord hath sent his angel, and hath delivered me" (Acts 12:11).

After considering his situation, Peter came to the house of Mary. Now, we must keep in mind that this was the home where the Saints had gathered to pray for Peter's release. It was the night before Herod was going to bring Peter before the people. In my mind's eye I picture a group of people praying without ceasing, desperate for the Lord to hear and answer their petition. The killing of James was fresh in their minds; they knew what would happen to Peter if he went before the Jews. After having already lost one Apostle, they must have cried with particular earnestness unto the Lord, pleading that somehow Peter would be saved.

I love what happened next. Peter approached the gate of Mary's home and knocked. Inside the home, a woman named Rhoda heard the knocking and came to investigate. It was the middle of the night, the condition was precarious, and obviously the Saints knew they were not safe from Herod and his soldiers. I am certain Rhoda was extremely nervous about who might be standing outside the door. So she listened at the gate to see who was there. "When she knew Peter's voice, she opened not the gate for gladness, but ran in, and told how Peter stood before the gate" (Acts 12:14).

It makes me giggle knowing that Rhoda left Peter, a wanted man, standing outside in the dark in a city that was unsafe. She left Peter, who had just escaped from prison, standing on the porch. In her gladness she forgot to invite him in!

When Rhoda ran to tell the other Saints that Peter was on the porch, they did not believe her. They told her she was mad. They didn't have time for her distraction; they were busy praying for Peter's release. But Rhoda would not back down from what she knew. So the Saints decided that Peter must have already been killed and that it was his angel standing on the porch. I find it interesting that within that very moment the Lord had already answered their prayers—they just didn't realize it.

Meanwhile, Peter stood waiting and knocking at the door.

Finally they opened the door, and when they saw him there they were astonished. Great worry turned immediately into great rejoicing. I imagine this is a story the Saints laughed about for many years after the experience. How, in the darkness of the night, Rhoda had listened to hear the voice of the one who approached the gate. How, in her gladness, she had forgotten to let Peter in. How all of them had discerned that it couldn't possibly be Peter, but must after all be an angel. And how, in unexpected and unanticipated ways, their prayer had been answered—but they hadn't recognized it until they opened the door and saw Peter standing there. Suddenly, after all, it was a good day (see Acts 12:1–16).

This story teaches an interesting lesson on prayer. Sometimes we are so busy praying for the answer we want, in the way we envision it will happen, that we almost miss the answer the Lord is sending us. Although we are praying without ceasing, the answer almost goes unnoticed.

Our Father is completely aware of our need and the situation we are in. I love this thought from Elder Jeffrey R.

Holland: "Some blessings come soon, some come late, and some don't come until heaven; but for those who embrace the gospel of Jesus Christ, *they come.* Of that I personally attest" ("'An High Priest of Good Things to Come,'" 38; emphasis in original).

Throughout our lives, there will be times when we find ourselves praying without ceasing. Heavenly Father hears those prayers. It is important for us to remember that sometimes, instead of sending the answer we want, He sends us the answer we need. When our eyes and our hearts are open to recognize those answers, we will be led to see good days.

To see a good day . . . learn to recognize the answers you need.

My heart had great experience.

ECCLESIASTES 1:16

Chapter Seven

MY HEART HAD GREAT EXPERIENCE

Sometimes when I am struggling to see good days, I try to remember a lesson from a wise man named Solomon. Just after King David died, Solomon, his son, prepared to become king. The night before Solomon was to be made the king, the Lord appeared to him in a dream. He said to Solomon, "Ask what I shall give thee" (1 Kings 3:5).

Carefully, Solomon thought through the situation he was about to be placed in. He was worried that he would not be equal to the task because he was young, and he wasn't exactly sure what he was doing. He was overwhelmed at the thought of how many people he would be serving. Think about this for a minute. If you had been in this same situation, what you would have asked for? Solomon asked, "Give . . . thy servant an understanding heart" (1 Kings 3:9).

The Lord was appreciative of Solomon's request. He answered, "Because thou hast asked this thing, and hast not asked for thyself long life; neither hast asked riches for thyself . . . ; but hast asked for thyself understanding . . . ; behold, I have done according to thy words: lo, I have given thee a wise and an understanding heart" (1 Kings 3:11–12).

There have been many times in my life that I have followed Solomon's example and prayed to have an understanding heart. Experience has taught me that this gift is not easily maintained; it is one that requires great effort and practice. But I take comfort in a verse of scripture written many years after Solomon requested this humble gift. In the book of Ecclesiastes, which some scholars have attributed to Solomon, we read, "And I gave my heart . . . yea, my heart had great experience" (Ecclesiastes 1:13, 16). I love the thought that in the beginning of his service Solomon asked for an understanding heart, and that many years later, perhaps it was he who wrote that his heart had great experience.

How do we give our hearts great experience?

Looking back at my own life, I can see that the greatest experiences my heart has ever had have involved understanding and service of one kind or another. On the days when I am struggling to see a good day, I try to find someone I can serve. This practice has led to some of the sweetest experiences of my life. Most include moments that have helped me to see a good day.

Some of us are born with a gift for serving. My next-door neighbor is like this. She is quick to observe ways that she can serve, and most often her acts of service are anonymous.

Others of us learn to serve by watching the example of another. I am like this. The greatest lessons I have learned about service have come from watching others, particularly my mother. I have heard her tell others that she learned how to serve by watching her mother. I hope that somehow my own children will learn this talent, that they will grasp hold of this gift that has been passed down for generations in our family.

The lessons my mother taught me have proved invaluable. She has stretched the capacity of my heart. From her I have learned to drop everything and be there when someone is in trouble. I have learned that bringing in dinner is not always the right answer—sometimes a casserole *is* what is needed most, but it is important to consider carefully and take the time to listen for the best way to answer a call for help. One of the most important lessons my mother taught me is that "In the quiet heart is hidden / Sorrow that the eye can't see" ("Lord, I Would Follow Thee," *Hymns*, no. 220), and how important it is to offer love before we judge someone. Sometimes just having an understanding heart is the greatest act of service we can perform. It allows our heart to have a great experience where otherwise we might have an awful one. It allows us to see the good, and to help others to see it too.

In the early years of our marriage, my husband used to travel out of town for three days every month. I had three young children at the time, and I hated sleeping in our apartment without him. So, on the day Greg left, I would pack us all up for a mini vacation, and we would go stay at my mother's house, twenty minutes away.

I will never forget one of these occasions when I had slipped away to my mother's for my mini vacation. Sometime since our previous month's visit, my parents' next-door neighbors had acquired a large, howling dog. Every time a car passed by, it would set the dog off. The dog particularly hated the lights of the cars that came down the street during the middle of the night. I know this because it barked all through the night, every time a car passed by. I was up all night, and so were my children, listening to the barking.

The next morning at breakfast I said to my mom, "You have got to do something about that dog."

"What dog?" my mom asked.

I looked at her incredulously. "The dog next door! It was up barking all night last night! Didn't you hear it?"

My mom just kept eating her breakfast as I ranted on. "I know that it is against the law to let a dog bark outside after ten o'clock at night, so you could call the pound and they would send someone out who would give them a ticket and that would solve the whole problem," I told her. (My mind had been active all night trying to come up with solutions; this seemed the most logical choice.)

My mother just kept eating her breakfast.

Finally I said to her, "Does the dog not bother you?"

"I don't hear the dog," my mom replied.

"How could you not *hear* the dog?" I asked, fearing that my mother was losing her hearing, or possibly her sanity, I wasn't sure which.

My mom patiently explained that a few weeks earlier, the neighbor had called her on the telephone. "I am calling to apologize for my dog," the neighbor said. "I know it must be a bother to you and your husband. But you need to know that I have a son, whom I adore, who is going through a really hard time right now." She explained that the counselor they were working with had suggested they get a dog to see if that would give her son something to live for, and somehow it was working. "I am so sorry about the disturbance," she said, "but right now there is nothing else we can do."

Then my mom looked across the table at me and said, "So when the dog starts barking, I don't hear the dog. What I hear is, '*I have a son, whom I adore,*' and the dog just doesn't bother me anymore."

It was a profound lesson. I had been so quick to judge. I knew what to do. We would call the pound and the matter would be resolved. My mother had taken a different route. She had an understanding heart, and it had allowed her to see the good. Her willingness to love, rather than judge, had made a huge difference in the relationship between her and her neighbor. To this day, even though they now live miles apart, they are best friends.

I learned a lesson in that moment that was life changing. It altered the course of my life *for good*. My mother's experience taught me to have an understanding heart, and this lesson has allowed my heart to have great experiences of its own.

I love the way Peter describes the Savior: "Jesus of Nazareth . . . who went about doing good" (Acts 10:38). I want to live my life like that. I want to *do* good. Sometimes when people ask me how I am doing, I like to reply, "I'm doing good," as a constant reminder to myself of what I *want* to be doing. I want to be *doing good,* just like the Savior did.

On days when you are having a hard time seeing the good, consider praying for an understanding heart. Give your heart a great experience. Look for someone you can serve. Maybe you will take in dinner to someone in your neighborhood. Perhaps you will pay for the groceries of the woman in line behind you. Or, you might just open your heart to see the good in someone who really needs that from you.

These will become heartfelt experiences that are precious and sacred to you. Through them you will see good days.

To see a good day . . . ask for an understanding heart.

ALL LARK JUST

OF YOUR SONS TO HAVE BREAK

SOME FRESH FLOWERS FOR YOUR LIV

WRITE SOMEONE A NOTE 7 - FIND SOME

NDCHILDREN THAT YOU DIDN'T KNOW

WRITE ABOUT SOMETHING SPECIAL THA

EACH OF YOUR GRANDCH

AT LEA

Now this is my joy . . .

ALMA 26:37

Chapter Eight

LIST WHAT
YOU LOVE

I love simple pleasures. For me, a simple pleasure is anything that can make me feel joy instantly—a bowl of vanilla ice cream with raspberries and chocolate chips (especially if I'm eating it for breakfast!), bath salts, walking along the beach. Sometimes a simple pleasure can be found in the memory of an experience. After a movie, a vacation, or even Christmas break, I love to ask my family, "What was your favorite part?" Just remembering and talking about our favorites can bring joy and sometimes laughter instantaneously.

Simple pleasures can be a powerful tool in helping us to see good days. I remember visiting my grandma's home just before she died. She lay on her bed surrounded by pink pillowcases and a floral blanket. I sat in a chair next to the desk in the corner of her room. We talked about each of the pictures that had been carefully placed on her writing desk. Hanging on the wall next to the desk was a typed list in a frame. I asked my grandma what it was for.

She explained to me that when my grandfather had died almost thirty years before, she had really struggled getting through the day. Sometimes she couldn't get out of bed because she was overcome with so much sadness. She prayed that she would find a way to make it through each day, and she felt prompted to write down some things she loved to do. She thought of thirty things, one for each day of the month. They were simple things, including "invite one of your sons to breakfast," "have an ice cream cone," "find out something about one of your grandchildren that you didn't know before," "watch the sunset," "feed some ducks," "take a different route home." She planned to do one every day. She went to bed each night looking forward to what the next day would bring. That was how she made it through life without my grandpa.

I found it interesting that even after she moved to a new place many years after my grandpa died, the framed

list still found a prominent spot in her home. It was something that helped her to see good days.

One of my favorite parts of the Book of Mormon is found in Alma 26, when Ammon is reflecting back over his mission experience with his brethren. I have spent many evenings with my husband and his mission companions as they have described their mission experiences and memories. I have seen the way their faces light up as someone begins a story, "Oh, do you remember when . . ." I have heard their deep, heartfelt laughter and, just listening to their memories, I have felt joy. I imagine this reminiscence of Ammon was much like that.

Within this chapter Ammon has made his own list, much like my grandmother's, except instead of simple pleasures, Ammon listed his experiences. As I read through Ammon's list of experiences, both the good and the bad, I find myself nodding in recognition. I remember those events, both the bitter and the sweet, because I have read the previous scriptural entries that led up to this moment. As Ammon recounts the individual details, sharing memories from his heart, my own heart becomes full until I too feel that "my heart is brim with joy" (Alma 26:11). What a wonderful experience Ammon and his friends and brothers had been through! What an amazing change of heart their converts had enjoyed! What heaven-sent blessings and miracles had surrounded them throughout!

As he lists each of these occurrences, Ammon eventually becomes so overcome with joy that he says, "Behold, who can glory *too much* in the Lord? Yea, who can say *too much* of his great power . . . ? Behold, I say unto you, I cannot say the smallest part which I feel" (Alma 26:16; emphasis added). Ammon's heart is so full, he finds himself almost speechless. And yet he continues on for almost twenty more verses, listing the things that he has loved about their experience.

My very favorite part of that chapter is contained in the last verse. After that long list of experiences and blessings, Ammon concludes with his testimony and then says, "Now *this* is my joy, and my great thanksgiving" (Alma 26:37; emphasis added).

This chapter teaches a very important life lesson—there is great worth in writing down the life moments that bring us happiness. Simply looking back on these experiences can fill our hearts until they are brim with joy. Maybe you could make a list of your own. What brings you joy?

You might consider looking through Alma 26 for ideas before you begin. From Ammon's example we come to recognize that all of the events on our list don't have to be sweet. Sometimes joy can come from heaven's resolution of bitter experiences. The list should include blessings and tender mercies from the Lord that you recognize in your own life. It might include times where you have been able to serve others. You could write a description of that service, and how you felt when the service was finished. Include within your list details of hard work, moments of rejoicing, and occasions that were significant. Your list might mention miracles and answers to prayer. Have you ever experienced moments when you had to step out of your comfort zone, moments when people laughed at your vision, or moments where you were afraid? List those, too. Next to those moments, try to recall times when you received strength beyond your own, comfort that only the Lord can give, or maybe an increase in charity. You might want to list some of the places you love—homes you have been to; areas you have visited; a spot of the world that holds irreplaceable memories. Include your testimony. If you look carefully, you will notice that Ammon did all of these things.

Several years ago I purchased a book titled *14,000 Things to Be Happy About.* The author started writing it in a tiny spiral notebook when she was in sixth grade. For twenty years she listed all the little things that made her happy. It is a 612-page list, single spaced, of happy things. My daughter, Grace, who happens to be in sixth grade, decided to start a spiral notebook of her own. Among others, her happy list includes "the sound of popcorn popping," "owls hooting from a tree," "when my friends stand up for me," "the warm feeling of hot cocoa," and "sleeping in my bed the first night after a trip."

If I were to start a list of simple pleasures, mine would include firework shows, a long walk at twilight, reading a book next to the fire, wading in a small stream, parades, a cup of French cocoa on the first day of snow, s'mores under the stars . . .

Lists are powerful. Perhaps you could start making your own list in a spiral notebook or typing it up to place in a frame. Consider your simple pleasures, your favorite memories, your best days. Share the beliefs that bring you happiness. List what you love. Within that list you will come to see the good days that make up your life.

*To see a good day . . .
list what you love.*

They that sow in tears shall reap in joy.

PSALM 126:5

Chapter Nine

SOWING IN TEARS—
REAPING IN JOY

One of the most awful places I have ever passed through is Baker, California. Don't get me wrong: I am sure Baker has its own redeeming qualities, but not in this particular memory. We were on our way from Utah to San Diego with my entire extended family. Greg and I were making the trip in a red Dodge Caravan. The week before we left, the air conditioning in the van had gone out. I had picked the van up from the repair shop the morning of our trip, packed it full, and we were off. The air conditioning worked fabulously until St. George, right on the southern border of Utah, and then it broke again.

Now, I love my husband, but he has this thing about

91

getting the job done right, and if people don't do it right the first time, they need to keep at it until they do. It's an unwritten policy. So, since the guy who had tried to fix the problem the first time was back in northern Utah, that meant we would have to survive without air conditioning until we were back home again.

Being without air conditioning is not so bad when you are driving along the coastline with your windows rolled down and a soft ocean breeze blowing through the car. It's an entirely different matter when you are driving through Baker, California, entrance into one of the hottest locations on earth: Death Valley.

About forty miles outside of Las Vegas, our family caravan stopped at a gas station. My kids piled out of our steaming van with red faces, limp hair, and damp, wrinkled clothing. After assessing the situation, my parents suggested that perhaps the kids should be split up among the empty seats in the other air-conditioned cars. There was a seat available for me as well, but I couldn't bear letting Greg make the journey alone—no one should suffer companionless through four hours of intense summertime heat at midday.

I talked Greg into buying several bags of crushed ice.

I put a bag on my lap, one under my feet, and one behind my neck. He loaded himself up as well, and then we were off. Like I said, I don't have pleasant memories of Baker, California. It's hot there. Excruciatingly hot. But we made it through, and now we have one more story to add to the list we are saving for our posterity entitled, "You Can Do Hard Things." It was a growing experience that came with several life lessons attached.

Looking back now, I can see the good parts of that day through lessons I was taught the hard way. I learned that I am married to a man who has high expectations for helping others succeed in their profession; I am married to a man who doesn't give up, who reaches the final destination even if part of the journey is grueling, challenging, even formidable; I am married to a man who believes in simple luxuries amidst the adversity, even if it is just a $1.49 bag of ice.

I have been thinking a lot about the unforeseen growing experiences we often find ourselves embarking on, and the life lessons that lie waiting within. I find it interesting that most often we don't get to choose the lessons we are about to learn. It seems that some teaching moments come unexpectedly; we can't always anticipate them. Sometimes the learning comes from experiences we would have avoided completely if we had only been given the opportunity. But through those experiences we learn that sometimes a particular set of circumstances is just what may be required to allow the needed growth to come.

These life lessons can be painful. In times of intense trial, we can actually feel ourselves being refined in the furnace of affliction. The process hurts. Sometimes we cry, weeping tears of question, wondering when the promised healing will come. But even in these times there is good concealed within—good that can be revealed only through that particular experience.

I learned a powerful lesson last summer from my friend Mary Ellen Edmunds. The lesson left an image in my heart that I won't ever forget. This is what she taught:

Many years ago, just after the fall of 2004, an amazing phenomenon happened. Throughout the parched desert country of Death Valley, just outside of Baker, California, many wildflower seeds lay dormant on the desert floor— just as they had for many years. The mountains that surround this desert country are relentless, formed in such a way as to trap the hot air and recirculate it throughout the valley, making this area one of the hottest places on earth.

On some summer afternoons the ground-level temperatures can reach up to two hundred degrees.

The flowers in this desert country are unique in the fact that the seeds they produce have an extra thick, waxy coating that allows them to hibernate on the desert floor for decades. The particular seeds that covered the ground in the fall of 2004 had weathered years of severe extremes as they waited, dormant, on the desert floor. And then, a once-in-a-lifetime experience happened. An early winter rainstorm came late in the fall. The rainstorms continued at regular intervals throughout the winter and into spring. This deep-soaking, gentle rain was essential. It began to wash away the protective covering that surrounded the seeds, and with time, they began to sprout.

In the spring of 2005 six inches of rain fell on the thirsty desert floor—three times the usual amount for this hot country. The conditions caused wildflowers that had been dormant for decades to sprout and take root across the valley floor, covering the stark white sand and black basalt mountainside with a burst of vibrant pink, purple, white, and yellow.

Experts said this kind of show is experienced extremely rarely.

It happened because the conditions were right. Suddenly a parched desert floor was covered with petals. The rain was essential to the process, allowing what had once lain dormant to take root and sprout, eventually blooming into a miraculous display of beauty.

Perhaps the same is true of our tears.

Somewhere within you there are seeds that have been carefully placed. These seeds are waiting patiently, dormant, for their time to come. When the conditions are right, they will take root. Sometimes the perfect condition that allows for the growth of these seeds is painful. Tears may be required. Slowly and gently these precious tears will wash away the protective covering that surrounds the seeds, and they will begin to sprout.

There is a unique beauty found in this kind of seed, for it blooms into a rare and precious blossom—one that you will treasure and protect; one that you will share with others when the conditions are right; one that would have lain dormant for your entire lifetime without this particular situation to allow for its growth.

The Lord knew about these kinds of seeds. He spoke of those who would tend carefully to their growth:

They that sow in tears
shall reap in joy.
He that goeth forth and weepeth,
bearing precious seed,
shall doubtless come again with rejoicing,
bringing his sheaves with him.
(Psalm 126:5–6)

There will be times when each of us will weep over the precious seeds hidden within us. On those days we will sow in tears. The tears are the only way to loosen the protective covering—the only way to allow this particular blossom to take root. In time the joy will come. Not replacing the pain or the tears, instead the joy will grow up out of the furnace of affliction, offering beautiful petals from what was once parched and barren ground. Our eyes will be opened to see the petals, and within them we will see the good.

The Lord will attend us through this sowing process. Through Him we will see great things if we are careful to watch for them: blessings that are sent specifically for our needs; coincidences that are really tender mercies from the Lord; miracles found within the ordinary events of the day. Looking back, we will recognize, "The Lord hath done great things for us; whereof we are glad" (Psalm 126:3).

We will see the good through our tears. And after the tears there will be joy. The sadness will not surround us forever.

We must remember that it is often through unexpected and even painful circumstances that we are led to discover the good that we otherwise would never see.

To see a good day . . .
remember that after the tears
there will be joy.

*Take heed . . . lest thou forget the things
which thine eyes have seen,
And lest they depart from thy heart
all the days of thy life:
. . . Specially the day . . .*

DEUTERONOMY 4:9, 10

Chapter Ten

SPECIALLY THIS
DAY

S ometimes in life we have what I like to call reaching
moments—moments when we have to reach beyond
our current circumstances to attain something higher.
These reaching moments come to us in different ways. A
new calling or position often places us in a reaching moment as we are stretched to reach our full potential. Times
of trial or adversity can cause us to reach out for help from
others. Private moments that test our faith often prompt us
to reach for the Lord.

Some reaching moments are like climbing up the rungs
of a ladder, each rung lifting us closer toward our goal.
Other reaching moments are like monkey bars. In these

situations we must keep hold of something solid as we reach toward the next rung.

During my fourth-grade year, I spent hours and hours on the monkey bars on our school playground. First I mastered the bars in the regular fashion, simply making it hand over hand from one end to the other. It took lots of time and practice. Often I would fall down halfway across the length of the bar because my grip on the rung behind was not strong enough to sustain me as I reached for the next. Once I had perfected that technique, I wanted to learn to skip a rung—swinging my body just enough to reach past the next rung in line to the one after that. It was hard work, but on the day I finally made it from one end of the bars to the other without slipping off to the ground, I was ecstatic! In my fourth-grade mind, calloused hands that were often sore from so much practice were a small price to pay for such an amazing accomplishment.

This monkey-bar principle is key to our success during some of the reaching moments of our lives. Every so often we will find ourselves in a circumstance that stretches us so greatly to our capacity that if we do not have a firm hold on what is behind us, we will not make it to where we are supposed to go.

An Old Testament story that illustrates this principle is

found in the book of Deuteronomy. As the people of Israel prepared to embark on their final journey to enter the promised land, Moses took time to give them great counsel. He asked the people to remember what they had been taught and then to live up to what they knew to be true so that they would never forget what the Lord had done for them. Within this sermon there was one key memory Moses wanted them to hold on to, even to cling to, as they prepared for the reaching moment that was ahead.

Moses said, "Take heed to thyself, and keep thy soul diligently, lest thou forget the things which thine eyes have seen, and lest they depart from thy heart all the days of thy life: but teach them thy sons, and thy sons' sons; *specially the day* that thou stoodest before the Lord thy God in Horeb, when the Lord said unto me, Gather me the people together. . . . And ye came near and stood under the mountain; and the mountain burned with fire unto the midst of heaven. . . . And the Lord spake unto you out of the midst of the fire. . . . Unto thee it was shewed, that thou mightest know that the Lord he is God; there is none else beside him" (Deuteronomy 4:9–12, 35; emphasis added).

Moses knew that the burning-mountain moment had been a life-changing experience for those who recognized what it was. He wanted them always to remember what their eyes had seen, never to forget that moment in their hearts. I love how Moses reminded them to remember *"specially the day."*

What are the special days in your life? Think of the moments when your testimony burned within. Elder Ronald A. Rasband encourages us to "think of the special experiences you have been blessed with in your life that have given you conviction and joy in your heart. Remember when you first knew that Joseph Smith was God's prophet of the Restoration? Remember when you accepted Moroni's challenge and knew that the Book of Mormon was indeed another testament of Jesus Christ? Remember when you received an answer to fervent prayer and realized that your Heavenly Father knows and loves you personally? As you contemplate such special experiences, don't they give you a sense of gratitude and resolve to go forward with renewed faith and determination? . . .

"In these days of worldly intrusions into our lives, when trials and difficulties may seem to engulf us, let us remember our own special spiritual experiences" ("Special Experiences," 11, 12).

These testimony-building moments are the memories that we must hold on to in our reaching moments—they will carry us from one rung to the next. Somehow we must learn to see the good in these special days, to remember them in our hearts, lest we forget.

I will never forget the day my oldest son, Caleb, received the packet containing his mission call. Caleb wanted to invite some of his friends to watch him open the call that evening at eight o'clock. I thought it was a great idea. He wanted to serve hot dogs.

Late in the afternoon I was making a list of who would be coming to make sure I had purchased enough hot dogs. Between grandparents, aunts, uncles, and cousins we were expecting just over forty people from our extended family. I called him up to ask how many more he anticipated. "I don't know, Mom," he replied. "I invited all of the Young Men and my leaders, my home teaching companion and the families we teach, the entire lacrosse team, and some friends from school."

I hadn't bought enough hot dogs.

Not only that, I wasn't sure if we could fit that many people into our house. At eight o'clock that night people started arriving, quickly filling the family room, kitchen, and front hall of our home. Once the doorbell finally stopped ringing, I ran upstairs to get my camera so I could record the minute when Caleb opened his call. As I walked out of the library,

I looked down the stairs at the rooms below—there were so many people you could no longer see the carpet, the tile, or even any of the furniture that fills up those three areas of our home. The house was completely bursting with people who had come to see Caleb open his call. As I turned to walk down the stairs I had an impression—*take a picture of this*—and so I did. Then I ran down the stairs so Caleb could open his call.

I don't think a mother ever anticipates correctly where her son will serve, so it won't surprise you to learn that I was completely shocked when Caleb announced he would be spending the next two years in Croatia. I didn't even know where Croatia was. After the hot dogs had been served and the well-wishers had returned to their own homes, we spent the evening searching the Internet to discover facts about a place we had never heard of.

Later that evening I lay in bed thinking of what we had learned. Running through my head were the thoughts of a mother worrying over the reaching experience she was about to send her son into.

Caleb's mission encompassed seven countries, of which only three were open for proselyting. The mission president was located in the country above the place where Caleb would serve. Within Croatia itself there were only twenty missionaries, and fewer members of the Church in the whole country than we had in our home ward. A missionary serving in Croatia could expect to baptize 0.4 people during his entire mission experience.

Needless to say, I was worried.

His would be a different experience from what I had anticipated, and I hoped we had prepared him well for the reaching moment. I knew there would be hard times—times of disappointment, rejection, and failure. I knew that he would have to learn a different definition of a successful mission experience, one calculated not by baptisms but by building. I knew there would come a time when he would wonder to himself, *What am I doing here, why did I come, and how will I make it through?* I felt the importance of helping him find strength to hold on to before he left, strength that he could cling to during the discouraging experiences that would lie ahead.

Almost immediately my mind was filled with memories from the past few years, family home evenings we had shared together, spiritual discussions that had taken place in our home. I tried to think of how I could help make those memories tangible in a way that might help him really hold on to them. I thought of the moments we had spent together preparing his mission papers, the moments leading up to the call, and *specially the day,* this day, when almost everyone he knew and loved had gathered within the walls of our home.

On this day he had carried that call in his hands for most of the afternoon, practically bursting with anticipation because he knew that the Lord's prophet had extended the call contained inside. On this day he had been surrounded by people who supported him, who would cheer him through every missionary experience he encountered in the next two years. On this day he had shared his testimony before he opened his call, the light shining in his eyes as he testified that more than anything in the world he wanted to serve the Lord. On this day he could barely wait to put on a suit and get to Croatia. On this day he knew where he was going and why. There wasn't a doubt in his mind. He was a confident and willing servant. Oh, how I wished that somehow, when he was miles and months away from here, he would be able to remember this day.

And then I remembered the picture.

Immediately my heart filled with gratitude for a loving Father in Heaven who knew in advance the thoughts of a mother's heart. I had been inspired to take a picture of that exact moment, of this day.

The next morning I had the picture printed in a size

that I could glue into the back of Caleb's scriptures. I knew there would be moments of discouragement when he got on his mission, times when he would wonder what he was doing and why he had come so far from home. When that happened, he could look back at that picture and say, *on this day, specially this day, I knew where I was going and why.* Then he would have something solid to hold on to.

Part of seeing good days is committing to memory what our eyes have seen and treasuring those moments in our hearts—never to be forgotten, always remembered. As we remember those special experiences, we will feel a sense of gratitude, and along with it, renewed faith and determination.

We must learn to recognize and never forget the good days, the important, testimony-building days of our lives. If we tuck those memories carefully within our hearts, then in moments of doubt, discouragement, or failure we can look back on those moments, *specially the days* when our testimony burned within, and see the good.

To see a good day . . . remember the special days.

109

For ask now of the days that are past, . . .
And ask from the one side of heaven
Unto the other,
Whether there hath been any such thing
As this great thing is,
Or hath been heard like it.

DEUTERONOMY 4:32

Chapter Eleven

IN EVERY PARTICULAR

One of the things I admire most about Nephi is his optimism. From the very first chapter of the Book of Mormon we realize that his view on life was completely different from that of his brothers. Laman and Lemuel saw everything from a cup half-empty perspective. Nephi's cup wasn't just half full; more often than not it was a cup that runneth over. We don't know all of the reasons why Nephi's point of view was different, but we do know one. Right at the beginning of his story Nephi tells us, "Behold, I, Nephi, will show unto you that the tender mercies of the Lord are over all those whom he hath chosen" (1 Nephi

1:20). Nephi knew how to see and recognize the tender mercies of the Lord.

Tender mercies are a constant theme filling the Book of Mormon. We are introduced to them in the very first chapter of Nephi and reminded not to forget about them in the very last chapter of Moroni, when Moroni says, "I would exhort you that when ye shall read these things, . . . that ye would remember how *merciful* the Lord hath been unto the children of men . . . and ponder it in your hearts" (Moroni 10:3; emphasis added). Learning to recognize tender mercies and to ponder them in our hearts can help us to see good days.

Elder David A. Bednar has defined tender mercies as "very personal and individualized blessings, strength, protection, assurances, guidance, loving-kindnesses, consolation, support, and spiritual gifts which we receive from and because of and through the Lord Jesus Christ" ("Tender Mercies of the Lord," 99). Many people consider this type of blessing a coincidence. I have learned otherwise. Often what we think of as a coincidence is really a tender mercy from the Lord.

I believe that there are two rules we can apply to a situation to see if it might be a tender mercy. The first rule is found in Doctrine and Covenants 46:15: "And again, to some it is given . . . according as the Lord will, *suiting his mercies according to the conditions* of the children of men" (emphasis added). From this scripture we learn that the Lord is able to tailor his tender mercies to the condition we are currently in.

The second rule is found in Alma 25:17: "The Lord had granted unto them according to their prayers, and . . . he had also verified his word unto them *in every particular*" (emphasis added). From this scripture we learn that the Lord is also aware of the particular needs that fill our lives. These two scriptures lead us to believe that if a coincidence is *suited to the condition* we are in, and fills *a particular need,* it might not be a coincidence after all. Instead, we should view it as a tender mercy from the Lord.

In the seventeenth chapter of Matthew we read about one of these tender mercy moments. The Savior was in Capernaum. While there, a tax collector approached Peter and asked if his master would be paying the tribute, or, in other words, the temple tax. Peter answered yes and then walked into the home where Jesus was. Jesus asked Peter, "What thinkest thou, Simon? of whom do the kings of the earth take custom or tribute? of their own children, or of strangers?" Peter answered, "Of strangers." So Jesus replied, "Then are the children free" (Matthew 17:25–26).

It must have become instantly clear to Peter that the temple was the house of God and the Savior was the Son of God. Since earthly princes would obviously not pay a tax on their own home, of course Jesus should not be expected to pay taxes on His Father's house.

The Savior understood the particulars of the financial situation they were currently in. He also knew the condition of the hearts of those who came collecting. With those two things in mind, He answered Peter, "Notwithstanding, lest we should offend them, go thou to the sea, and cast an hook, and take up the fish that first cometh up; and when thou hast opened his mouth, thou shalt find a piece of money: that take, and give unto them for me and thee" (Matthew 17:27).

Consider the circumstance and particulars of this scripture story. Elder James E. Talmage wrote: "We cannot doubt that what Jesus had promised was realized. . . . The knowledge that there was in the lake a fish having a coin in its gullet, that the coin was of the denomination specified, and that that particular fish would rise, and be the first to rise to Peter's hook, is as incomprehensible to man's finite understanding as are the means by which any of Christ's miracles were wrought" (*Jesus the Christ*, 384–85.) The Savior knew instantly how to answer the particular need of the circumstance they were in, and a tender mercy was orchestrated.

Tender mercy stories are not just recorded in the scriptures. If our eyes are open to see and recognize tender mercies, we will find that they are regular occurrences that make up the ordinary details of our lives.

I have a dear friend whose six-year-old son was diagnosed with bone cancer. Understandably, the family was devastated with the news. On numerous occasions I talked with my friend about the changes that they were facing. Of particular distress to her was the thought of the number of school days her son would miss as he struggled through the intensive chemotherapy routine.

Her son was in kindergarten, and I remember my first thought being, *You don't even have to attend kindergarten in Utah. It won't matter how many days he misses.* But as I listened more carefully, I realized that it wasn't his progress in kindergarten that mattered to her. What mattered was that he was missing the ordinary, day-to-day things that all of the other kids his age would be participating in. I could feel her heartache.

We researched what could be done to remedy the situation. Ty Ty would have to miss a lot of school, considering both the days he would be in the hospital and the days he would be at home sick from the chemotherapy. When he did attend school, his body would be in a very fragile state, which meant he would require extra care and supervision. After his parents counseled with the administration of the school, it was decided that Ty Ty qualified for an aide.

But finding the aide proved to be difficult.

Ty Ty needed someone who was willing to be very flexible, working only on the days he was well enough to do schoolwork, either at home or at the hospital, and accompanying him to school when he was able to go. At most, it would be two hours a day. The days would not necessarily be consistent; sometimes the job would require only one or two days a week. The aide would find out his or her schedule the evening before each day. It was a hard position to advertise for.

The school suggested that my friend ask her family members or friends to see if they knew someone who would fit the criteria, but the schedule was not conducive

for anyone she knew. As the weeks wore on without a potential candidate, my friend became discouraged. We decided to pray that we would be able to find someone who
could meet Ty Ty's needs.

Several days later I received a phone call from one of
my neighbors. She wanted to know if I could write a letter
of recommendation for her. Writing letters of recommendation is something I do for people frequently, and I told her
I would love to, but I needed to know a little bit about the
job she wanted to apply for so that I would know what to
write. "I am not sure," she told me. "I am looking for a really
flexible position, not more than ten hours a week. I don't
want to work every day. I will need random days off every
so often, and working in the morning hours would be best."

I couldn't believe it. This was exactly what we were
looking for. I told her, "I can do better than a letter of
recommendation, I can offer you a job." I shared the circumstances of the situation and she accepted immediately.
Then she said, "This is so interesting. I have felt prompted
to call you every day this week."

Later that day I was speaking with my friend about
how the events had played out and the tender mercy
that had unfolded before our eyes. I said to her, "In the

moments that you will face during this upcoming year
when you wonder if the Lord is aware of you and of your
situation, you need not doubt. Just remember this moment
and you will be reminded instantly that the Lord is acutely
aware of you and what you are going through." To this day,
it still amazes me that the Lord was so aware of the particulars and conditions of her circumstance. Recognizing these
tender mercies along the way has helped my friend to see
good days in the midst of some really bad ones.

Learning to open our eyes and recognize the tender
mercies that fill our lives will help us come to understand
a very important reality: "What [God] had promised, he
[is] able *also* to perform" (Romans 4:21; emphasis added).
God does not just give us promises. He is able *also* to perform those promises according to the conditions and the
particular details of our life.

Sometimes when I find myself in awe of a carefully
orchestrated tender mercy, I am reminded of a scripture
found in Deuteronomy that says, "When thou art in tribu-
lation, and all these things are come upon thee, . . . if thou
turn to the Lord thy God . . . ; (for the Lord thy God
is a *merciful* God;) he will not forsake thee. . . . For ask
now of the days that are past, . . . and ask from the one

side of heaven unto the other, whether there hath been any such thing as this great thing is, or hath been heard like it?" (Deuteronomy 4:30–32; emphasis added).

Our God is a merciful God. He is able to send tender mercies into our lives according to our conditions, suited to the particular challenges we face. If we watch for them, they will become miracles amidst the ordinary details of our lives. They are oftentimes unexplainable, but that doesn't make them less real. We can lift the hearts of those around us as we "go home . . . and tell them how great things the Lord hath done for [us]" (Mark 5:19). We must learn to recognize these moments in the days that are past, and from the one side of heaven unto the other, to view the great things that happen in the ordinary details of life as tender mercies from the Lord, and, in so doing, to see good days.

———◆———

To see a good day . . .
recognize the great things as tender
mercies from the Lord.

God, even thy God, hath anointed thee
with the oil of gladness.

HEBREWS 1:9

Chapter Twelve

THE OIL OF
GLADNESS

Annie Grace Sabin was born at 3:45 p.m. on Wednesday, March 30, with a heart that was broken. Silence filled the room as the doctors, nurses, and Annie's parents waited to see if she would breathe. Finally they heard a tiny cry, and then she was quickly passed to the newborn intensive care unit, where she would fight to live.

In the midst of Annie's trials, her mother posted a blog that touched my heart. She wrote:

"The past two days have been the most difficult of my life. . . . Annie came out of surgery Friday night and things looked good. Her chest tube output seemed to be slowing and she appeared to be stable. However, within a few hours, she took a turn for the worse. . . . We woke up Saturday morning with very heavy hearts as we knew that if things did not change for the better very soon, our Annie would not be with us much longer. . . .

"There has been one moment in this experience with Annie that, in a way, sums all of it up for me. . . . Her heart rate was sky high most of the day and after calling for the crash cart twice and administering every medication possible, the doctors were running out of options to help her. I had listened to her heart beat between 200 and 240 beats per minute on the monitor for most of the day. Around 5:30 that evening, the surgeon came to her room and within a few moments, he was preparing to go inside her chest. I was in shock. I could not believe that they were not asking us to leave the room (I definitely didn't want to leave, but until this point in time we had never even been allowed to be in the room when they changed her bandages). We stepped outside her door, so we would be out of the way, but I was able to watch everything that was happening in that room.

"When Dr. Burch removed the bandage from her chest, I immediately saw her tiny beating heart. It wasn't until then that I really knew how scary this all was. Even though I had listened to her heart beat all day, I didn't grasp how fast it was beating until I saw it with my own eyes. It was as if her heart was panicking, beating faster than I could bring my two fingers together in sync with it. Seeing it helped me to understand why a heart beating that fast could not sustain life. There was simply not enough time for it to fill with blood and pump it to the body. I watched the doctor hold her heart in his hand and lift her lung in an effort to place another chest tube that he believed could help her. While he was doing this, her heart slowed down and the monitor showed that it was beating in the 140s. Perfect! I was so excited and felt sure that he had fixed whatever the problem was, but by the time he replaced her bandage and stepped into the hall to talk to us, her heart rate was again above 200.

"I was so frustrated and expressed to him that he must have placed the tube in the wrong spot, as her numbers had improved for a time but were now worse again. He very patiently explained to me that this had nothing to do with where he had placed the tube. It was actually the pressure of his hand on her heart that had helped it to calm down and slow to a more reasonable rate. He told me that it was unreasonable for someone to hold her heart in their hand until she got better (I volunteered, but he gently declined my offer).

"I think about this day often. Partly because it was such an unbelievable experience, but mostly because it has come to symbolize what my Heavenly Father has done for me during these last several months. Panic has become a familiar feeling for me. There is no better word to describe how I have felt on so many occasions with Annie. My heart has ached and raced and been filled with dread and fear for her. At times, I have been almost overcome with panic, but each time this happens, I feel like Heavenly Father reaches down from heaven and holds my heart in His hands until I am able to feel peace again. When the feeling of panic returns, I don't sense the disappointment that you might expect from a Father who has told His child again and again that all would be well if they would just trust Him. He just reaches down and holds my heart. Tonight my heart is in His hands and I am at peace" (anniesinmyheart.blogspot .com, Sunday, June 27, 2010; used by permission).

In the heartbreaking experiences of our lives, when we are heavyhearted, careworn, and weary, where do we turn for peace? In those reaching moments I find myself searching for the Giver of Every Good Gift; the High Priest of

Good Things to Come; the One Who Upholdeth with His Hand (see Psalm 37:24).

He is Jesus Christ.

I am drawn to Him.

There is a place within my heart that only He can fill. A need within my soul that only He can succor. A longing that only He can soothe.

When I yearn for the peace that only He can bring, I am reminded of a scripture found in Hebrews that teaches of a time long ago, before we were born. The scripture says of the Savior, "Thou hast loved righteousness . . . ; therefore God . . . hath anointed thee with the oil of gladness" (Hebrews 1:9). I have spent a great amount of time pondering on what the "oil of gladness" might be.

I think of what oil has the ability to do. It has a way of seeping into places that are hard to reach—permeating, soothing, and even healing. I know from personal experience that the Savior is capable of doing all these things. Isaiah tells us that the Lord was sent to "bind up the brokenhearted . . . ; to comfort all that mourn" (Isaiah 61:1–2). The Lord knew that there would be seasons when each of us would mourn, periods in our lives when we would experience a spirit of heaviness. In those trying times, we must leave our hearts open, allowing the sadness to fill the moment but knowing that the Savior's oil will heal our hearts and that, in time, we will experience gladness again.

The scriptures teach us that not only was the Savior anointed with the oil of gladness, He was also anointed to give "the oil of joy for mourning" (Isaiah 61:3). When our broken hearts are in heaven's hands, we must turn to the Savior, who has been anointed with the oil of gladness—who gives the oil of joy. He will soothe our hearts. He will help us heal. And when we are finally ready to see good days again, He will show us how.

Through Him, gladness will come.

To see a good day . . . let the oil of gladness permeate your heart.

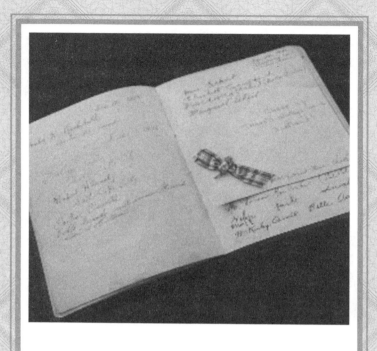

. . . a day of gladness . . .
and a good day

Conclusion

THE HAPPY
BOOK

I n a hand-carved drawer of the antique desk that sat in
my grandmother's living room, a hidden treasure was
carefully tucked away. Sometimes when I would go and
visit, my grandma would pull out the treasure and let me
gently look through its pages. It was a brown leather journal that she had received as a gift from her Aunt Margaret
in 1937. She called it her happy book because it brought
her happiness every time she glanced through it.

The book is filled with happy thoughts. The very first
inscription is dated December 1937, and was written as a
housewarming wish from my Great-Aunt Margaret to my
grandmother. It is one of my favorite entries in the journal:

129

To the New House

May your listening walls hear the sounds of
Gay laughter and harmony.
If sorrow comes
May your rooftree be a place
Where comfort and peace can be found.
May you come with joy and never leave this
      house with heavy hearts,
And may you always be able to look back
      and say:
"It was a happy time!"
May sunshine be on your path.
May the years bring you friends who are
      stalwart and brave.
May blessings many and sorrows few
Be your lot.
That is my wish for you.

Carefully inscribed on the rest of the pages in the journal are the signatures and often additional thoughts of everyone who visited my grandmother's home from December 1937 through June 1997—over sixty years' worth of memories. When I was younger, one of my favorite things to watch for on the pages of the journal was my dad's name. It appeared for the first time in 1947, carefully written by my grandmother—Dad was then two years old.

Ten years later he signed his name himself in cursive. He was twelve. By 1960 his signature took on quite a bit of personality. It made me giggle. Written carefully on the other pages are Christmas dinner entries, notes from the basketball squad my grandpa coached at East High, and signatures from women who came for an MIA teachers party. Some people composed poems; others wrote down quotes; many just signed their names. Reading through all of the messages Grandmother's guests left taught me things about my grandparents that I hadn't known before.

When my grandmother died, each of the grandchildren got to choose something to take home as a memory. I chose the happy book. It's been almost ten years since she passed away, and I still love thumbing through the pages of Grandma's leather book. It makes me happy. The thing I love most about that old leather journal is that it contains a record of my grandmother's good days.

In the book of Esther, after everything had finally calmed down, the Jews celebrated. Their enemies had been slain, Haman and his ten sons had been killed, and throughout the land the Jews gathered to rejoice in their deliverance and victory. I love the description of this event: "a day of gladness . . . and a good day" (Esther 9:19).

Looking back at my grandma's happy book, I think she could have written that at the top of every page—a day of gladness and a good day. It is the perfect description of what her journal contains. Days of gladness. Good days. At the end of each day, she chose to remember the good part.

If you are someone who hopes to see good days, I would like to share one last idea that will make a significant difference to your success. It is spoken of first in Luke, in a scripture that is familiar to all of us: "And Mary hath chosen that good part" (Luke 10:42). It is referenced again in the Book of Mormon when Lehi, who is at the end of his life, says, "I have spoken these few words unto you all, my sons, in the last days of my probation; and I have chosen the good part" (2 Nephi 2:30).

The good part was something they *chose*.

I believe that we too can choose the good part every single day. The choice is a powerful one that will change our life—*for good*. It will help us to let go of the common adage "have a good day" and instead learn to "see a good day" because seeing the good is something we have chosen to do.

Perhaps, at the end of each day, as you go over the things you have experienced, you could choose to remember the good part. Maybe you could start your own happy book and fill it full of days of gladness and good days. If I were to visit your home and you allowed me the opportunity to write a message in your happy book, I know exactly what it would be—a reminder of the twelve happy thoughts we have talked about in this book, and a hope that they would somehow fill your heart and become a way of life.

This would be my heartfelt inscription:

To my newfound friend,

May you see a good day.

May your perspective be governed by
Light, laughter, and discernment.

If mountain moments come your way,
May you rise above and continue your journey
Knowing the Lord is with you.

May the breaking of each day
Find you on your knees.

May you live after the manner of happiness.

May your focus lead you to understand
That God is in the details.

As you pray each day for the answer you want,

LOVE LIFE, AND SEE GOOD DAYS

May you remember that He might send
The answer you need.

May your heart have great experience.

May listing what you love allow you
To recognize your joys.

If sorrow comes your way,
May you sow in tears
And reap in joy.

May you always remember the important days
Of your life,
Specially the days
When your testimony burned within.

May your eyes be quick to search
From one side of heaven unto the other
And recognize the great things
As tender mercies from the Lord.

May the oil of gladness permeate your heart.

May every day be a day of gladness
And a good day
Because you have chosen the good part.

This is my wish for you.

Emily Freeman

Fall 2011

Acknowledgments

With much gratitude . . .

To Amy Sabin, Sarah Smith, and Verda Dallon for welcoming me into the conversation that is your life.

To Fred, who introduced me to the Story Tree on the Trail of Wonder in Coalville, Utah—many of these pages were crafted under those shady boughs.

To my mom, Megan, and Grace, who accompanied me through many of the learning moments that fill these pages. It is our crazy excursions that make life especially sweet. I won't ever forget our early-morning drives through Pleasant Grove, the dandelion fields of Heber, or the long walks to the beach for French fries on a stick and pink cotton candy.

To a great team at Deseret Book. Emily Watts, who was my editor second and my friend first. Your love of words and your gift for phrasing are truly remarkable. Jana Erickson, who has a unique vision for making words on paper become an experience for the heart. Laurel Christensen, cheerleader extraordinaire, for your suggestions, ideas, and support. Shauna Gibby, thank you for welcoming my thoughts. Tonya Facemyer, I won't ever forget you at the back of the chapel with this galley held close to your heart. You are good to me.

And, after all, to Greg, who married me even though I was a rainbow chaser, and who has found as much joy in that pursuit as I do.

SOURCES CITED

Bednar, David A. "The Tender Mercies of the Lord."
Ensign, May 2005.

Clegg, Gayle M. "The Finished Story." *Ensign*, May 2004.

Edersheim, Alfred. *The Life and Times of Jesus the Messiah.*
2 vols. New York: Longmans, Green, & Co., 1900.

Holland, Jeffrey R. "'An High Priest of Good Things to
Come.'" *Ensign*, November 1999.

Kimball, Spencer W. "The Breaking of the Day Has Found
Me on My Knees." *Ensign*, February 2004.

———. "The Role of Righteous Women." *Ensign*,
November 1979.

SOURCES CITED

Monson, Thomas S. "Finding Joy in the Journey." *Ensign*, November 2008.

Rasband, Ronald A. "Special Experiences." *Ensign,* May 2008.

Talmage, James E. *Jesus the Christ.* Salt Lake City: Deseret Book, 1977.